VISUAL BRIDGES
for
SPECIAL LEARNERS

by the same author
Playing, Laughing and Learning with Children on the Autism Spectrum
A Practical Resource of Play Ideas for Parents and Carers
Julia Moor
ISBN 978 1 84310 608 1
eISBN 978 1 84642 824 1

of related interest
Activities for Adults with Learning Disabilities
Having Fun, Meeting Needs
Helen Sonnet and Ann Taylor
ISBN 978 1 84310 975 4
eISBN 978 1 84642 962 0

Music and the Social Model
An Occupational Therapist's Approach to Music with People Labelled as Having Learning Disabilities
Jane Q. Williams
ISBN 978 1 84905 306 8
eISBN 978 0 85700 636 3

Promoting Social Interaction for Individuals with Communicative Impairments
Making Contact
Edited by M. Suzanne Zeedyk
ISBN 978 1 84310 539 8
eISBN 978 1 84642 783 1

Active Support
Enabling and Empowering People with Intellectual Disabilities
Jim Mansell and Julie Beadle-Brown
ISBN 978 1 84905 111 8
eISBN 978 0 85700 300 3

Group Music Activities for Adults with Intellectual and Developmental Disabilities
Maria Ramey
ISBN 978 1 84905 857 5
eISBN 978 0 85700 434 5

Caring for the Physical and Mental Health of People with Learning Disabilities
David Perry, Louise Hammond, Geoff Marston, Sherryl Gaskell and James Eva
Foreword by Dr Anthony Kearns
ISBN 978 1 84905 131 6
eISBN 978 0 85700 225 9

VISUAL BRIDGES
for
SPECIAL LEARNERS

A Complete Resource of 32 Differentiated
Learning Activities for People with Moderate
Learning and Communication Disabilities

JULIA MOOR

Jessica Kingsley *Publishers*
London and Philadelphia

First published in 2013
by Jessica Kingsley Publishers
116 Pentonville Road
London N1 9JB, UK
and
400 Market Street, Suite 400
Philadelphia, PA 19106, USA

www.jkp.com

Library of Congress Cataloging in Publication Data
Moor, Julia, 1966-
  Visual bridges for special learners : a complete resource of 32 differentiated learning activities for people with moderate learning and communication disabilities / Julia Moor.
    pages cm.
  ISBN 978-1-84905-301-3 (alk. paper)
  1. Learning disabled--Education. 2. Special education--Activity programs. 3. Individualized instruction.
4. Visual learning. I. Title.
  LC4818.M66 2013
  371.9--dc23
                           2013010992

British Library Cataloguing in Publication Data
A CIP catalogue record for this book is available from the British Library

ISBN 978 1 84905 301 3
eISBN 978 0 85700 689 9

Printed and bound in Great Britain

*Dedicated to my inspirational students past and present
and my treasured son Robin, whose own challenges in life have kept
me seeking ways to understand and support atypical thinkers.*

Contents

Introduction

At the start of my career teaching adults with learning disabilities and communication challenges, it became quickly apparent that if the curriculum content was to be based on meeting the learners as a collection of individuals and tailoring activities to suit their interests and abilities, then the planning for these sessions would be high on resources and labour intensive. Differentiating learning to such a high level often led to several 'micro lessons' within one class and a continual battle to pull students together for group activities. Over the years, through discussions and observations of other such contexts, it would appear my colleagues across many settings were experiencing the same 'juggling act' – how to be fully inclusive yet maintain a group approach. On top of working out such high levels of differentiation we are also recording and evidencing our students' progress to fit learning aims tied to accreditation at pre-entry or foundation level. Our students are not 'average' learners; they often have complex communication difficulties, yet can display skills in specific tasks that don't reflect a generic cognitive 'stage'. Many students are learning outside nationally accredited pathways, students for whom belonging to part of a learning group means more than achieving a certificate. These are learners with significant 'delay' who are at a stage in life when they are ready and able to engage in learning at a level meaningful to them. These learners often find themselves in community education or attending organised learning in day services. Teachers, tutors and trainers have many more tools now than I had two decades ago; the internet can offer session plans and printables in abundance, but this very abundance can become overwhelming, especially to staff new to the profession.

My hope is that teachers, trainers, tutors, care support managers and in-house activity providers will all benefit from this practical and creative set of differentiated lessons written for adults with moderate learning disabilities in a variety of settings. Each session is comprehensively described in detail with printable resources, learning aims and suggestions for differentiation and extension. The activities are designed around real outcomes rather than 'time fillers', with a focus on addressing the communication barriers that a mixed group of special learners face in the classroom. The sessions can stand alone or be used, as the book suggests, as a block of themed activities around four domains: Learning Skills; Cooperation and Teamwork; Self-Awareness and Awareness of Others; Exploring Representation, Language and Literacy. This resource is the culmination of tried and tested activities delivered over several years to a variety of learners. The activities have been specifically designed to:

- enable all learners to attend to the same learning topic/language and images by offering several ways to differentiate or develop activities

- encourage cooperation between learners in groups

- develop individual communication

- develop confidence and motivation by enabling successful creative results

- stimulate imaginative input

- develop concentration, memory and recall.

As new activities have been developed and evaluated, students have continually challenged me to keep these fresh, motivational and, above all, accessible. Based on my experience that many adult learners with learning disabilities contend with communication difficulties to varying degrees, all of the activities are accompanied by visual material to act as cues and references as well as communication starting points in themselves – bridges to fill the gap between spoken language and cognition. Wherever possible, the activities are linked to everyday life skills to remind learners where and how they will benefit from participating in the activity and developing specific skills.

Each activity has a visual marker near the title, which indicates the primary mode of engagement:

- visual

- auditory

- tactile

This allows an instant assessment by the teacher to the suitability of the activity. For many of the activities there are also suggestions for how to include students with visual impairments. The activities are explained to support the teacher to differentiate the difficulty level of the task, breaking it into stages where necessary so that an activity can be scaled down or up and pitched correctly to motivate all learners in the group to attend to the same theme. Repetition is the key to practising learning to concentrate, listen and recall, and many of the group activities described in the book can be repeated as a regular 'warm up' or 'close down' to sessions. Materials can be changed for variety, though it is wise to be mindful that although repeating activities with the same materials can get 'boring' for regular students, for students having difficulties with concentration and recall a higher level of rehearsal can enable success and further encourage students to engage.

The enclosed CD has all the printouts in full colour, as resources in colour offer more information to support understanding and encourage participation. Though it can be time-consuming, to preserve these resources through lamination means less printing and wastage in the long run. If individual worksheets are laminated, students could complete these with dry wipe markers and the page be photocopied as a progress record before being wiped clean. However, when time and resources are running low the majority of these 'printables' are also included here in the book in black and white for instant reproduction.

I hope that any one of the activities could work as a springboard to enable a raft of further learning to be developed by the teacher using the principles of including visual bridges wherever possible and adopting a multifarious approach to presenting ideas. Ultimately, I hope this resource inspires and challenges teachers to take a more creative look at delivering learning to their very special group of students.

SECTION 1

Learning Skills
Senses, Process and Recall

 All photocopiable sheets that accompany these activities can also be printed in colour from the CD at the back of the book. This icon denotes any sheets that can be found on the CD, but are not included in the book.

Introduction

Adult learners with learning disabilities attending group sessions often struggle to filter out background noise, process and interpret information and maintain concentration. They may be out of practice in engaging with their wider surroundings because they are overwhelmed by sensory overload or de-motivated by increased passivity. These concentration difficulties alongside communication challenges affect the processing and retention of new information and the ability to be taught fresh skills. Activities that practise those skills required to 'learn' can be, and indeed should be, hands on, fun, and engage all learners at an ability and communication level suited to them as individuals.

As teachers, tutors, trainers and session leaders we all know that motivation is the key to enabling our students to maximise their learning potential. A mental checklist at the start of the session will help:

Do students understand why we are doing this activity? Have I explained how this skill can benefit them in everyday life?	✓
Have I controlled the difficulty of the task? Does the task challenge my more able students without overwhelming my less able students?	✓
Will I deliver the activity in stages to allow students to process clearly?	✓
Have I created communication opportunities for students to choose, ask, share and engage in any way they are able?	✓
Have I got plenty of visual information to support spoken ideas and instructions?	✓
Will students be engaged using a multi-sensory approach?	✓
Have I addressed all environmental barriers (e.g. student seating, sensory issues, lighting and sound levels)?	✓
Am I enthusiastic about the activity myself?	✓

A ticked list means a motivated student

The activities in this module aim to motivate students to think about how they take in the information around them and to help them practise discrimination through touch, sound and vision.

Thinking for ourselves is something that we as 'typical thinkers' take for granted. Adults with learning disabilities in care settings have restricted opportunities for making choices and taking control of their everyday lives and can often take a passive presence by observing, listening and 'doing' less for themselves than they may be able to.

Our learners can really benefit from practising concentration and recall skills. Enabling them to be successful at this in the classroom can lead to improvements in interacting within the wider environment of their lives... If we take in more of what's around us then we have more information to make choices.

Teachers are encouraged to explain to students why it is relevant to practise 'seeing' and 'remembering' not just useful facts but everyday significant information such as the location of things and places. By making the long-term benefits of engaging in the activities *relevant* and *meaningful* to the student, the teacher is more likely to encourage students to participate. It is often easy to forget that students attending lifelong learning need the significance of the activity explaining to them; we may feel they are keen to just *get on and do* and don't want to delay the process. For verbal students or non-verbal students with receptive language skills, it is always important to value the students' time and efforts by explaining in accessible language, and with clear and relevant examples, how working on a particular skill will help them in everyday life.

There are suggestions on how and when to create 'communication opportunities' and how to take a multi-sensory approach. Students will have the opportunity to practise processing and recalling auditory, tactile and visual information – all key skills to practise as we 'learn how to learn'.

The Learning Skills activities can either form a block of sessions or be used independently as part of a wider course to increase arousal and readiness to engage at the beginning of class.

1.1 Senses
Which Sense? A Group Warm Up

This mental and physical warm-up activity would work well at the start of a learning session to pull the group together, encourage learners to engage and get them ready for participation. I find that throwing a dice is something all learners can do with minimal support, making participants feel successful and motivated. The 'hands-on' nature of the activity motivates reluctant participants and sparks discussion in itself.

Aims

- Develop awareness of turn taking and own role within a group activity.

- Review and identify the five senses.

- Review awareness of representation (e.g. the picture of an ear represents listening).

- Create an opportunity for discussion; speaking and listening to peer group.

- Develop concentration and attendance to a task.

Resources

- A print of the dice template onto card (or paste it onto some card).

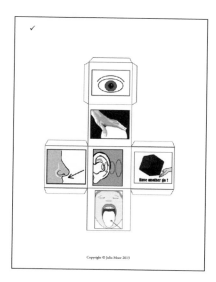

- Laminator (optional).

- A copy of the picture sheet for each participating student.

- A copy of the senses visuals for each student.

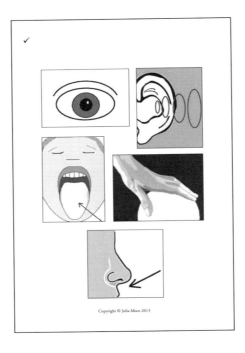

Prior to the activity

Assemble the dice by either printing it onto card or attaching to card with spray adhesive. Cut the shape out with scissors, *gently* score along all the straight edges using a craft knife and fold into a cube. Glue the tabs in place to make a secure dice.

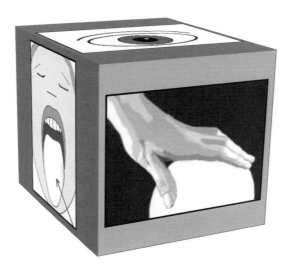

Cut out the separate pictures on the picture sheet and paste onto cardboard or laminate. This will make the activity easier to handle and durable to last for several sessions. Do this for however many students you have (i.e. one set per student).

Delivering the activity

Introduce the subject area by discussing that when we learn our brains are given the information around us through our senses. Provide each student with a visual sheet showing each of the five senses to start a general discussion. Do the students know which sense each picture represents? Explain to students that this 'information' can be sounds, sights, smells, etc…and that by spending some time thinking about which senses we use to understand the world around us we can begin to understand how we prefer to learn. We may discover we prefer listening to instructions or following pictures; we may discover that handling physical items helps us learn. For some students specific senses may be impaired so we may rely more heavily on others. We are taking in information all the time from light levels (what sense?) and temperature of the room (sense?) to the specific pictures (sense?) and sounds (sense?) we are listening to during the lesson. Provide the students with the picture cards and the dice and begin to take it in turns to roll the dice and announce the result (e.g. 'something you can taste').

Students around the table then select a picture (from their set on card) to hold in the air. The group leader then initiates a discussion around the result. Is there consensus between students/ disagreements/pictures that can apply to more than one sense? Remember this version of the game is a discussion generator; students are not playing to create a winner. Decide on how many throws each student gets – one each for a large group or two to three for a smaller one.

Conclude the activity with a discussion about student's individual learning preferences. This is a good way to generate ideas about how your students may prefer to learn. Who enjoyed the 'dice throwing' most? Listening to and participating in the discussions? Selecting pictures? They may even challenge you to present some 'tasting' activities!

Differentiation and development

- You may wish to provide a large beaker or box for students with motor skill difficulties to 'shake' the dice in.

- Similarly for these students make the picture cards easier to manipulate by pasting onto thick card and using sticky tack to attach the choice cards to the edge of the table.

- The activity can be used at a simpler 'matching' level. For students unable to select matching pictures to senses, print a second set of the senses visuals. The student then matches the correct visual to the one thrown on the dice in a straightforward 'same to same' match.

- For students requiring more of a challenge, there is a second set of cards:

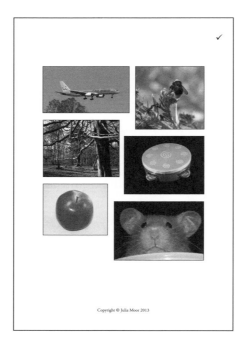

These students could use the second set alongside the first set to offer more choice during discussion. They could be asked to label verbally or write underneath each picture the senses used to process them. Students at a higher level of literacy could be asked to write adjectives under each picture to describe how it might feel/sound/look/taste/smell.

- A specific set of sensory cards can be made for students with visual impairments, as follows:

  ○ **Touch**: Glue a feather to card.

  ○ **Smell**: Soak a card in perfume (store in a separate plastic bag so that this doesn't make all the cards smell).

  ○ **Taste**: Stick dried pasta or wrapped boiled sweets to card.

  ○ **Listen**: Attach a small cat bell to card.

  ○ **Sight**: The student can think about which of the above could only be seen (sun/moon/stars/rainbow). How does your visually impaired student imagine this looks?

Students who would prefer playing the activity as a competitive game can 'post' their selected card into a box – the first to post all their cards wins.

The activity can be developed further by asking students to make their own set of cards, each with images torn from magazines. Remember to provide some images that only match one or two senses, for example a rainbow or thunder. Assess whether students know which senses apply to their selection by getting them to check it off against the sheet of senses visuals. Once each student has their own individual set of images the game can commence.

For students working on early literacy, substitute the picture cards for the word version.

✓	
Sea	Boat
Fish	Leaf
Bird	Music
Apple	Rainbow
Bee	Guitar
Mountain	Moon

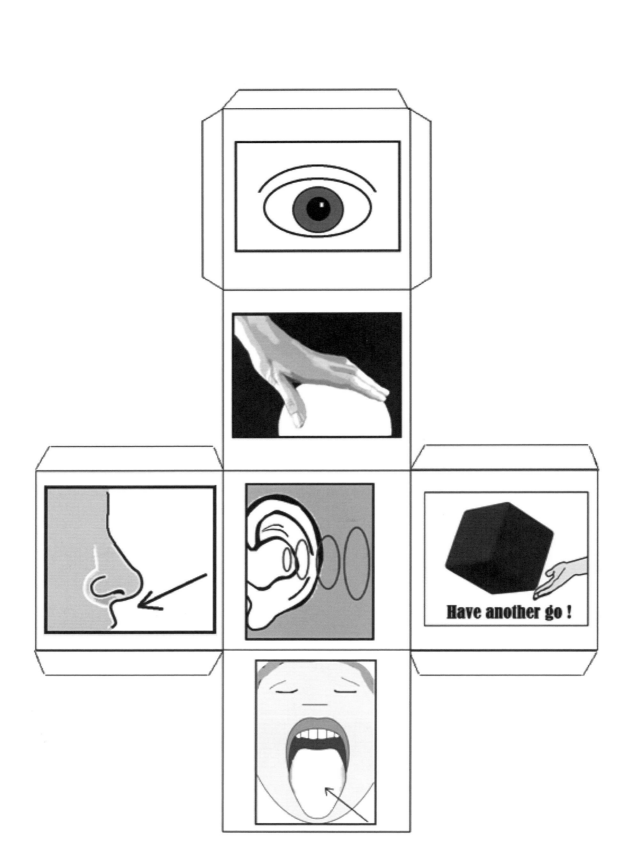

Have another go !

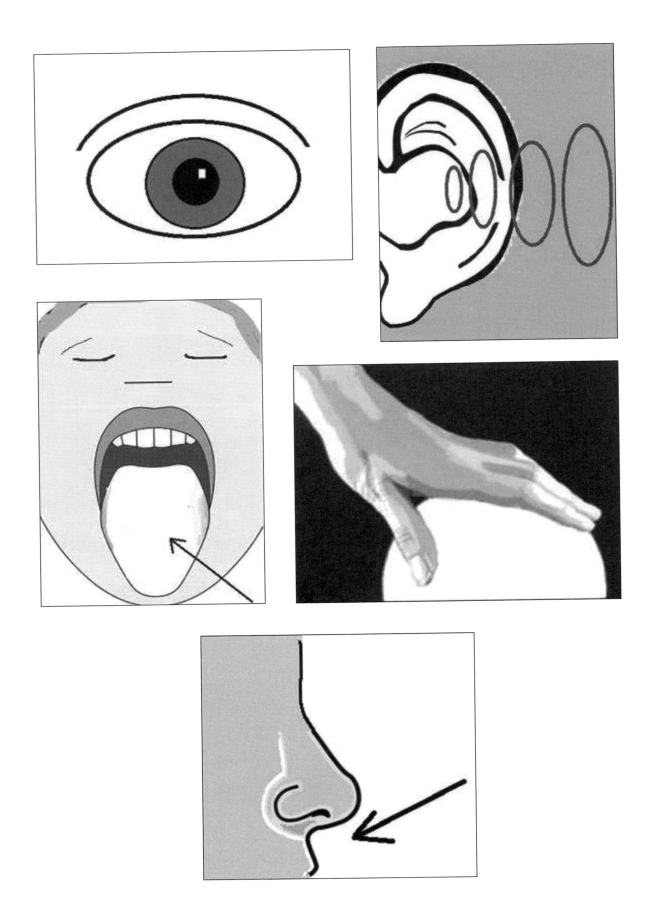

✔

Sea	Boat
Fish	Leaf
Bird	Music
Apple	Rainbow
Bee	Guitar
Mountain	Moon

1.2 Process
A Group Tactile Discrimination Game

This activity can be used with all learners, including those experiencing visual impairment or hearing loss, to stimulate communication and participation. It's a particularly good warm up for 'hands on' sessions, getting learners motivated to reach, touch and explore tactile material. Handling objects that can't be seen can challenge some students to take a leap of faith and is an opportunity for teachers to build bonds with their students through sensitive and supportive communication.

Aims

- Create an opportunity for participation.

- Develop awareness of turn taking and own role within a group activity.

- Focus concentration on discrimination by touch only.

- Develop awareness of representation (e.g. a picture can represent a touched item).

- Create the opportunity for developing adjectives.

- Develop motivation and confidence to explore using touch.

Resources

- A large cardboard box.

- A collection of everyday items with matching photos. (The picture sheet has a selection of items you could easily get hold of; you may choose to use all of these or just select and cut out the ones you have objects for.)

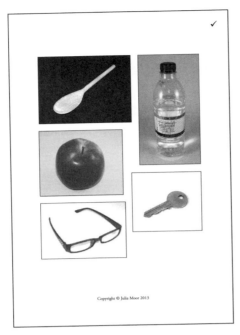
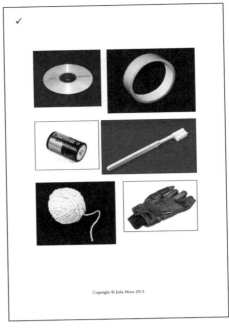

- A cloth to conceal the items going in and out of the box.

Prior to the activity

- Seal up the box and cut two circles into one side, large enough for the student to place a hand in each.

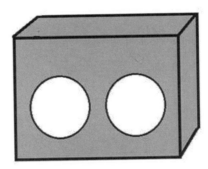

- Print picture sheets for each participating student.

- Print sheets for differentiation and development as described below.

Delivering the activity

Begin the session by assessing who is comfortable with touch and ask for volunteers to shake the hand of the person sitting next to them, and close their eyes while they are shaking hands. Ask the students who is shaking a warm hand and who has cold hands? Can they feel if the person is wearing rings or a watch? Is it a male hand or a female hand? Then they can open their eyes to check! Students uncomfortable with this may be able to shake the session leader's hand instead or could be asked to handle a neutral object such as an orange or a cushion. Ask the group why being able to 'feel' the world around us helps to keep us safe. If something feels too hot, or prickly, or sharp, what do we do? Talk about the kitchen and bathroom – hot taps and pans, sharp tins, and so on.

Explain that the activity is going to remind students how to become more aware of their sense of touch by describing an item that they will only be able to feel but not be able to see. Many students with learning disabilities need encouragement to reach out and explore using touch, so be patient and explain the activity, giving examples of some of the things they may expect to feel. Remember to tell students specifically that nothing will be wet/living/unpleasant. Review some descriptive words before you start the activity such as shapes, textures, and sizes; you may want to print off the 'adjectives prompt sheet'.

Set up the box at the end of a table with a 'hot seat' in front of it. Ask for volunteers to feel and describe the item (without naming it) to the rest of the group. The remaining students choose a corresponding item from the picture sheets in front of them. Now ask the 'feeler' to guess what the item is. When everyone has chosen, compare answers. Who was correct? Cover the box while you swap for a different item.

Differentiation and development

- For all students make sure the box is secured to the table (masking tape works well).

- If this set-up is too difficult for more than one student, or students are not mobile enough to move to the 'hot seat', then try placing items one at a time into a drawstring bag that can be passed around.

- This activity specifically assists students to place themselves in the position of having a visual impairment and helps create a sense of value for those students with a visual impairment who may feel in the minority.

- For pre-verbal students, everyone has a turn to feel and then point to their choice on the picture sheet, keep changing items and passing the box or bag around the table until everyone has had two/three turns.

- Signing students (Makaton) may wish to sign the item to the group. Remember to pick items that you know your students have signs for.

- For students developing verbal communication, ask them to describe the function of the object to the group. What do you do with it? What do you use it for? Where would you find it?

- For students developing written language, replace the picture sheet with the written label sheet.

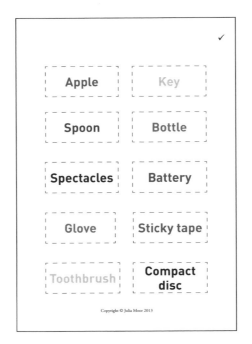

- This activity can be used to familiarise students with the labels and feel of resources and materials they would be using for a particular course (e.g. cookery/specific crafts). Create your own picture sheets by photographing the items that students will be handling on a regular basis and use as a regular warm up to the session to cue students to engage.

- For students on literacy courses, the activity can be used to extend and develop use of adjectives. Ask the 'feeler' to only use three adjectives from the adjectives prompt sheet. Each student then has to guess what the item is (either with or without the picture sheet to offer possibilities).

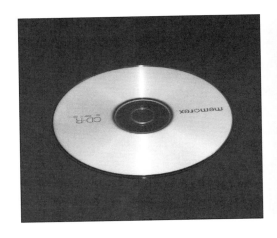

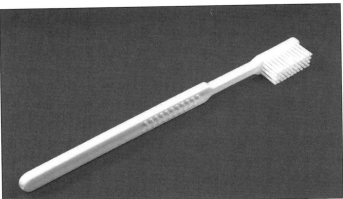

✓

Apple	Key
Spoon	Bottle
Spectacles	Battery
Glove	Sticky tape
Toothbrush	Compact disc

Long

Fluffy

Soft Warm

Flat

Tiny

Smooth

Hard

Sharp

Bumpy

Thick Cold

Round

Thin

Flaky

Dry

Short

Square

Crooked

Curly

Fat Damp

Dusty

1.3 Process
A Sound Discrimination Activity

Learning new skills often demands concentration on a great deal of speech content. For students struggling to process spoken speech this can lead to concentration difficulties and confusion over expectation. This activity is designed to help students concentrate and process sound information other than speech. Learners will need to practise filtering out background noise, comparing sounds to each other and making links between pictures representing sounds.

Aims

- Create an opportunity for participation.

- Create an opportunity for group discussion.

- Focus students on discriminating between sounds.

- Develop concentration and attendance to task.

- Create an opportunity to identify and explore problems and solutions around 'noise issues'.

Resources

- 6 empty jars with screw tops.

- Marbles/several coins/several pencils/buttons/tea bags/dried pasta.

- A copy of the picture checklist for each student.

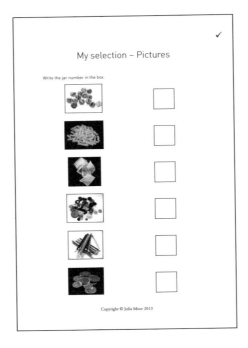

Prior to the activity

- Obscure the contents of each jar by wrapping a sheet of paper around and securing with tape. Fill each jar with each of the six contents above. You may wish to secure the lid onto the jar with tape. Write a number (1–6) clearly on each jar.

- Gather printed materials for Differentiation and development as described below.

Delivering the activity

Start the session by discussing sounds. How do you know what a sound is if you can't see its source? Ask students to shut their eyes and listen to the sounds around them…what can they hear? Talk about specific sounds that they may be able to discriminate. Discuss sound likes and dislikes (including the teacher's own preferences). Why is it useful for us to be alert to the sounds in the environment? Does it help us keep safe? What about traffic noises/road crossings/railway station announcements? Describe how you are going to practise working out sounds that you can't see, and explain that each jar has an object inside to identify just by the sound it makes when it is shaken.

Allow a set period of time for students to listen to the jars one at a time and then write the jar number against the picture on the sheet that they think matches the sound. Ask students to try not to shout out what they think the sound is. Present all the jars together on the table to encourage students to wait to take their turn to shake each jar, cooperate with each other and to swap jars when they have finished.

When everyone has completed their sheets, encourage them to vote on the outcome then empty the contents of each jar one by one into a tray.

Differentiation and development

- If students are unable to write numbers then wrap a different coloured paper around each jar and ask students to colour in the number box with the matching colour instead.

- As a simpler one-to-one activity, the student could simply stick the chosen picture to the jar.

- For students developing literacy, print off the words checklist and ask students to match these first to the pictures before then identifying the sounds.

- If jars are too tricky for students with physical disabilities to handle, try using sealed cereal boxes. Cut out the pictures and stick each one onto a sheet of A4 paper and spread over the table. The student can then place the box onto the picture that he or she feels is the correct sound.

- Help students with visual impairments differentiate between jars by adding raised dots to represent the jar number. There are several ways to do this: use plastic counters stuck to the jar, or try 3D fabric paint (allow this to dry for 24 hours before you need to use the activity). Allow time for visually impaired students to handle the objects after they have guessed to check if they were right or not.

- Invite students working at a higher level of verbal communication to think about adjectives to describe each sound. Write ideas (adjectives or memories) on the sheet of 'thought clouds' and place a photo in the middle to create a mind map associated with a particular sound. Ask students to share their ideas with the rest of the group, for example:

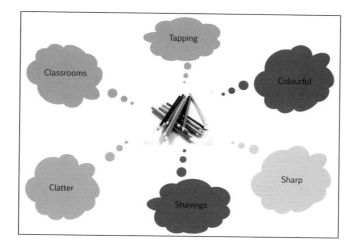

- Students may then wish to identify sounds they don't like (e.g. other people's loud music, loud talking, too much chatter, supermarket sounds, building works) and think about solutions. For example:

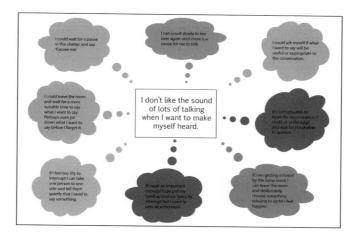

- Use the list of 'noise problems' or students' own ideas and assemble them into a 'solutions mind map' like the one above.

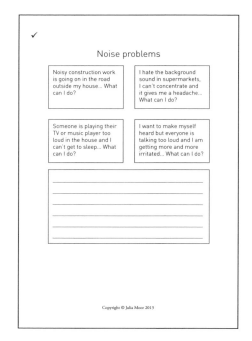

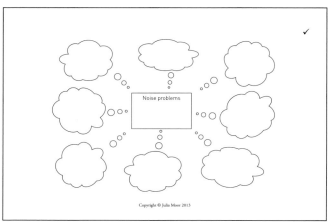

My selection – Pictures

Write the jar number in the box.

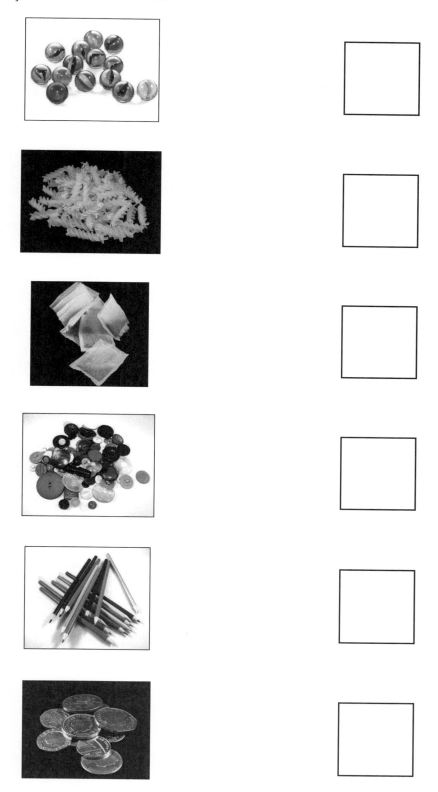

✓

My selection – Words

Write the jar number in the box.

Coins ☐

Pencils ☐

Marbles ☐

Buttons ☐

Tea Bags ☐

Pasta ☐

Paste picture here

Noise problems

Noisy construction work is going on in the road outside my house... What can I do?	I hate the background sound in supermarkets, I can't concentrate and it gives me a headache... What can I do?
Someone is playing their TV or music player too loud in the house and I can't get to sleep... What can I do?	I want to make myself heard but everyone is talking too loud and I am getting more and more irritated... What can I do?

_____

_____

_____

_____

_____

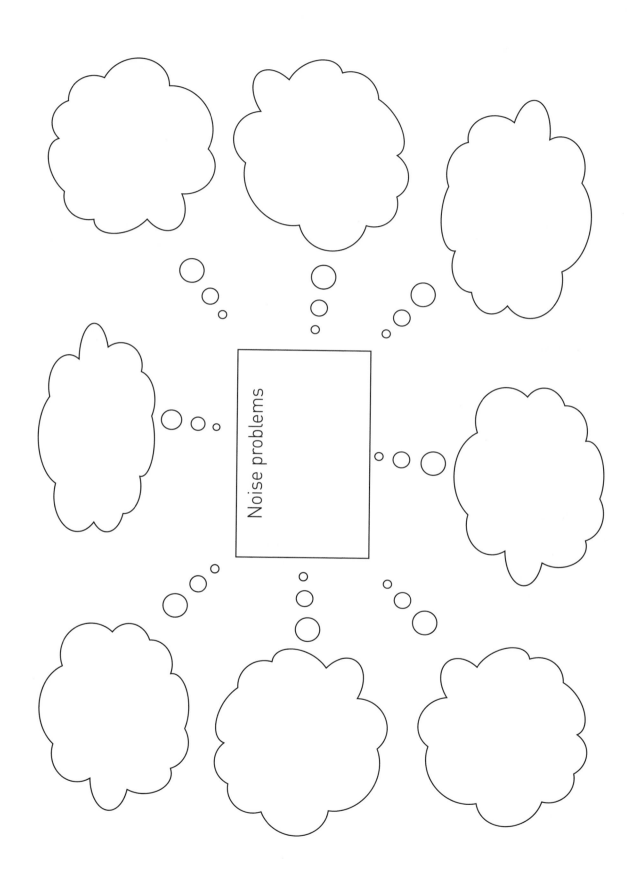

Noise problems

1.4 Process
Rhythm Bingo – Sound Memory

I often use bingo-style games to introduce groups to new topics and ideas; the rules are consistent and easy to generalise and the format is instantly recognised by learners. This group bingo activity can be made to include students with visual impairments and is a good ice breaker for a new group.

Aims

- Listen and attend to other group members.

- Discriminate between fast and slow rhythms.

- Practise concentration, memory and recall.

- Opportunity to practise recognising numbers 1–6.

- Opportunity to take part in wider discussion about rhythm and memory.

Resources

- Choose and print off a set of bingo cards appropriate for the ability level of the group/individuals (there are 8 cards for up to 8 players). Some cards are picture rhythms (i.e. with the number of hand claps illustrated) with some of these cards only showing low numbers (2–4).

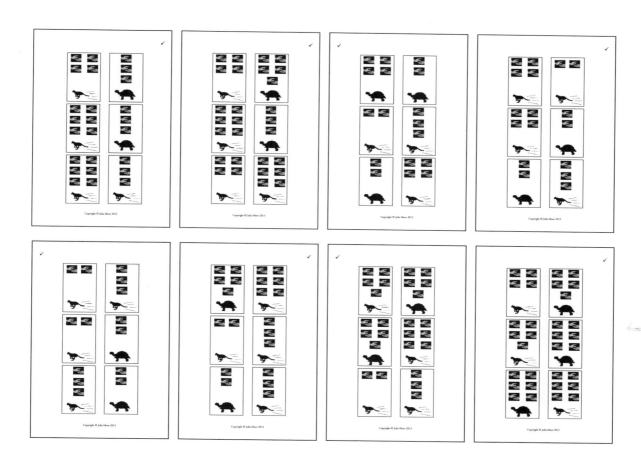

- For students able to recognise written numbers use these cards instead. These 6 sheets are available on the CD component of this book only.

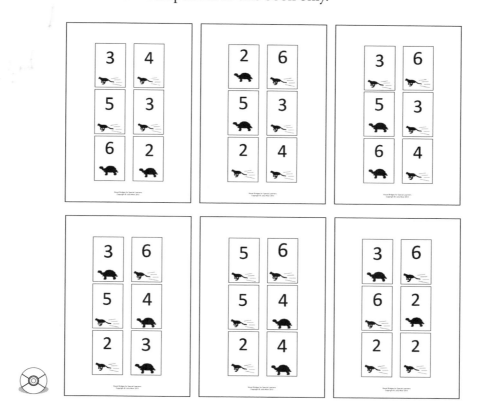

- Picture cards for tortoise and cheetah, one for each student.

- 4 dice printouts: low and higher numbers in picture form of clapping hands and low and higher numbers in number form. As with the cards, the dice with numerals can be found on the CD component of the book.

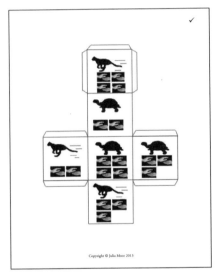 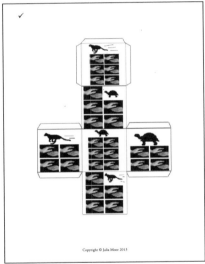

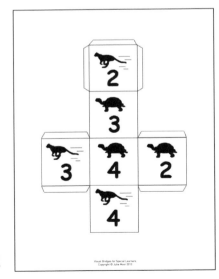 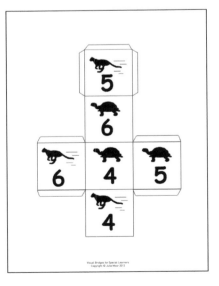

- Optional musical instruments (maracas/drum/tambourine) as required for students who may find clapping difficult (see Differentiation and development).

- 6 plastic counters for each player (milk tops work well), or dry wipe markers or bingo pens if players are just marking off on paper.

- Optional tactile cards for visually impaired students (see Differentiation and development).

Prior to the activity

Print off (onto thin card) the two dice showing numbers or the two dice showing the pictures of clapping hands depending on the your students' ability to recognise written numbers. *Gently* score along all the straight edges using a craft knife and fold into a cube; glue the tabs in place to make a secure dice.

If time and resources are not available to create the dice, print off and cut out the 'Bingo call cards'. Students can then select these at random out of a box.

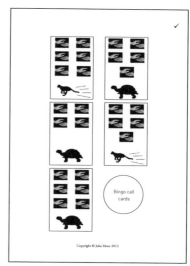

Print a bingo card for each player on paper or laminate, depending on whether you intend to use it again or not.

Create tactile cards if required for visually impaired students.

Delivering the activity

Announce to the group that you want them to remember these numbers:

62   25   22   42   21

Now create a two-minute delay by discussing something unrelated, and then ask who has remembered the numbers.

The chances are most students will be struggling to recall them.

Try again, but this time clap a rhythm to the numbers: 622 522 422 1. Make the rhythm again, then comment on how it sounds like a train rhythm. Now ask the students if they can remember the numbers; with the added rhythm this should be a lot easier.

Has anyone spotted that it sounded like a train?

Explain that the session will be about making and recalling rhythm because being aware of rhythms can help us recall all sorts of things from numbers, to names, to music. Rhythm can also help us get words out when we speak. At this point students may wish to discuss the rhythm of the sound of their own names. Ask the group what three fast claps would sound like, and four slow claps and so on. Create opportunity for volunteers to make a rhythm for the rest of the group.

Show the students the picture card of the tortoise and ask them to clap five times at the speed that a tortoise walks.

Now show the cheetah picture and ask them to clap five times at the speed of a cheetah.

Now look at how that would look as a picture by showing students the bingo selection cards or assembled dice.

Let the students choose an A4 playing card each (fan them out) and count out six counters each. If you have a varied ability group then choose appropriate cards for each individual (e.g. picture cards or number cards).

Familiarise the students with the pictures; do they know what they will be listening out for? Show the selection cards and demonstrate if you feel some players are not sure what is expected of them.

Let the game begin… Select the first rhythm bingo call card in one of several ways (choose one that best fits your group):

- Students take turns to select a small picture card from a box and clap the rhythm for the rest of the group.

- Students take it in turns to choose and throw a dice (low numbers 2, 3, 4 or higher numbers 4, 5, 6).

- Number selection cards 1–6 on the reverse; students working on numeracy throw a small dice and select the matching numbered card.

- The session leader makes and claps the selection.

- The session leader may need to support counting for some students.

The players now listen to the rhythm, check their card and place a counter (or mark with a dry wipe marker pen or bingo marker) if it matches. The first to place a counter on all six squares shouts 'Bingo' and wins. For players with more than one of the same rhythm sequence on their cards they must wait for it to be selected separately each time before they can place a counter.

Differentiation and development

- There are already two versions of the game, one using cards and a dice with written numbers and one using cards and a dice with pictures of clapping hands for students able to count but who may have difficulties with written numbers.

- For students who may struggle with all of the above, the game can be played as a simple 'match same to same activity' by printing off a second set of the bingo cards to cut up and offering them to the student to match up when a particular rhythm is selected.

- A tactile playing card can be made for visually impaired students using an agreed tactile marker for fast and slow (on this sample we used a bead for fast and a pom-pom for slow). The number was represented by dots of three-dimensional fabric paint. For Braille users you could use a dot formation for F and S (if you don't have access to a Braille embosser). Although preparing such a resource can be time-consuming, if the game is to be played regularly then this will become a highly valuable inclusive resource. Allow plenty of time for visually impaired students to familiarise themselves with the resource so that they have fully processed what it represents.

- Depending on the severity of the visual impairment you could take this a step further by attaching the six squares separately (using hook and loop dots) onto a larger card; students can then just pull off and remove the appropriate square.

- Some students may find placing counters on the card too fiddly or may need somewhere specific to place them. Sticky dots made from 'hook and loop' fabric with one piece on the playing card and the other on the counter means they don't slide about. If you play this style of game lots of times with your students, provided all your counters have either all 'loops' or all 'hooks' then you need only add the corresponding dots to your new cards and you will have a full set of counters ready for a different game! If you have laminated your cards then students may enjoy using dry wipe markers and crossing off their squares as you would in actual bingo. Similarly, if you are playing the game as a one-off, just printed on A4 paper, you may like to supply students with bingo pens.

- You may find it useful to provide maracas/castanets or a drum for those students with physical limitations that might make clapping too difficult.

- After the bingo game, students could take turns to clap or make their own rhythm sequence for the rest of the group to copy. You may also want to experiment with adding a third dimension of soft and loud – students then have to retain the number, speed and volume of the claps.

- Talk about fast and slow rhythms in everyday life; you may want to search for some 'free online sound effects' – anything from raindrops to a dripping tap to feet walking on gravel. You could even work on making a sound bingo game with your students using sound clips downloaded to a disc and asking students to find/make images to match the sounds.

- Try playing fast and slow music and discuss the feelings and emotions that this evokes. Remember to supplement discussion with picture support, such as smiling/thoughtful/sad faces, to help students who need to supplement their communication to express their own ideas.

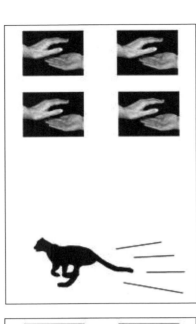

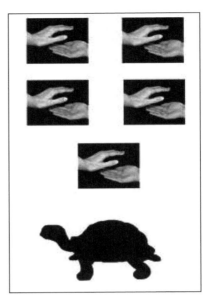

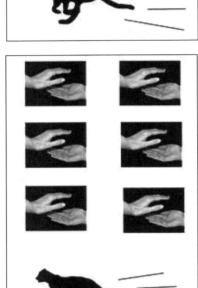

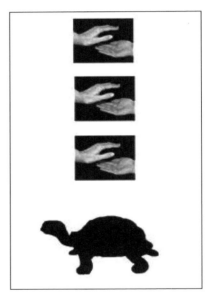

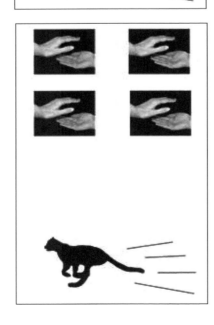

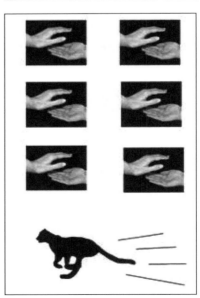

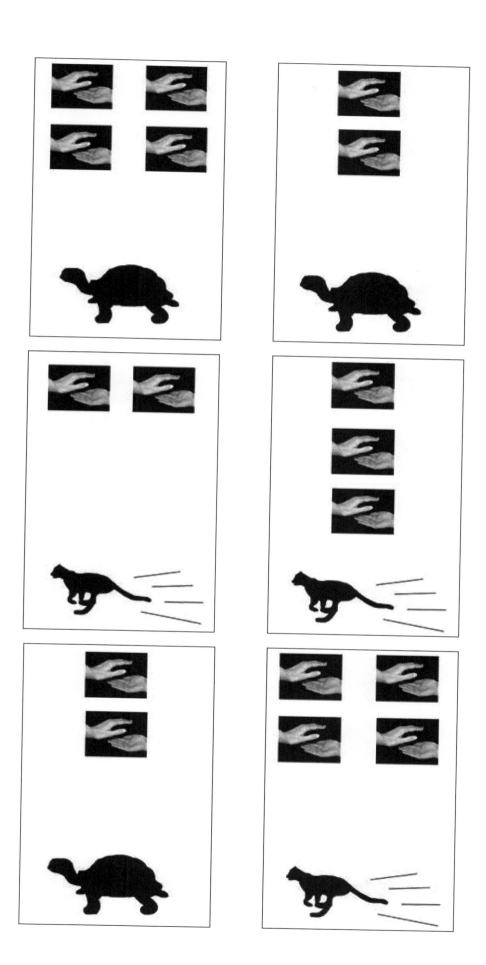

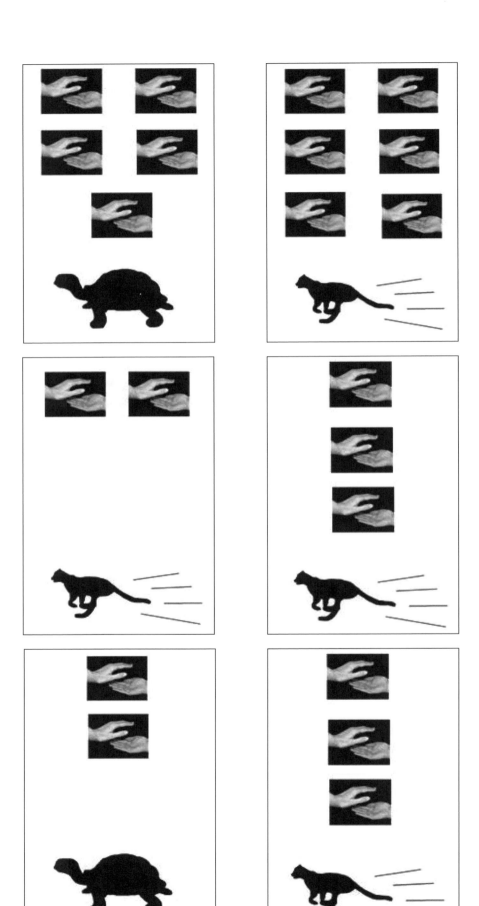

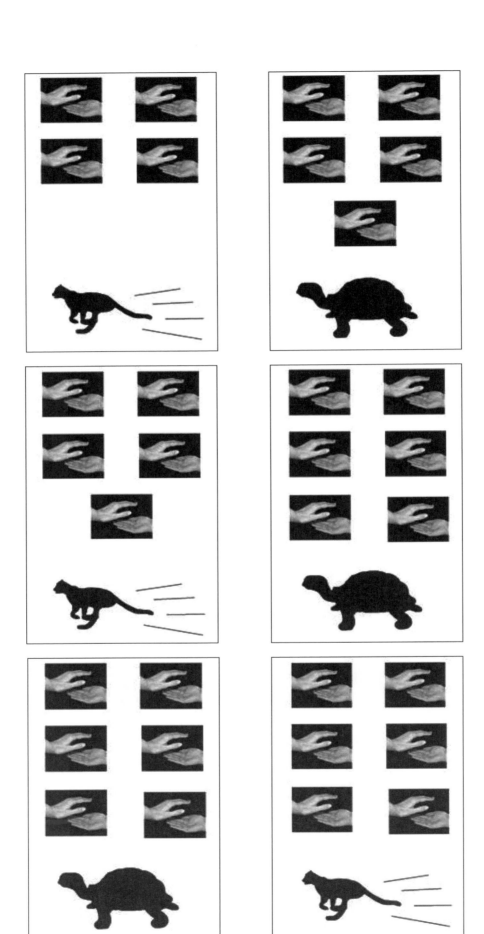

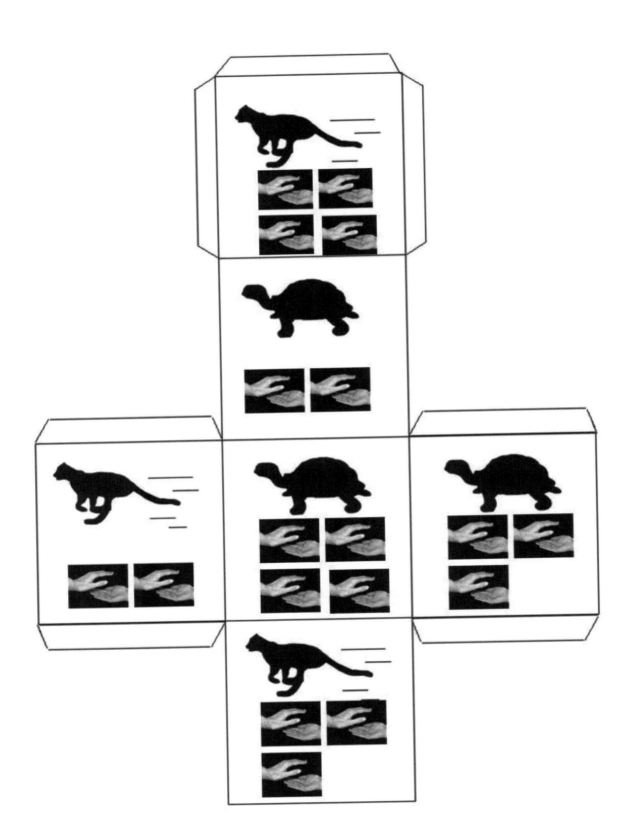

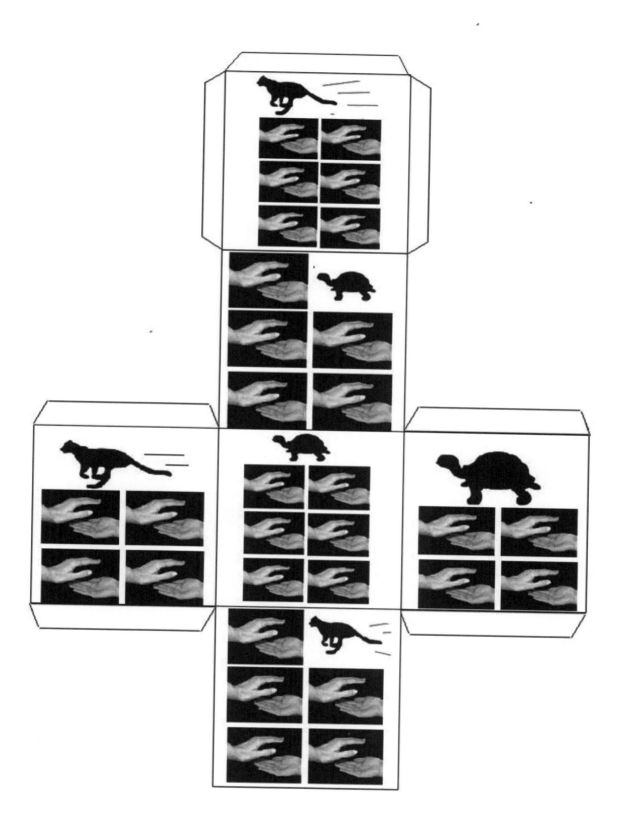

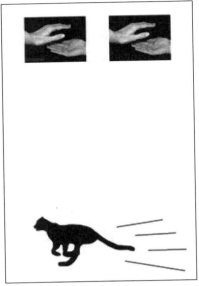

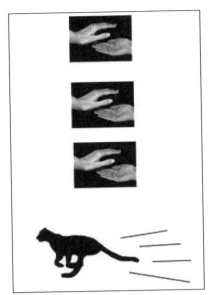

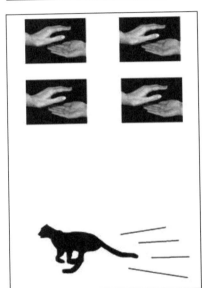

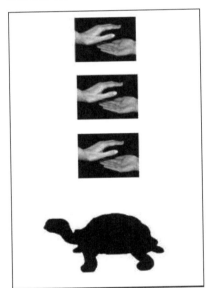

Bingo call cards

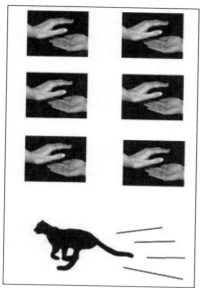

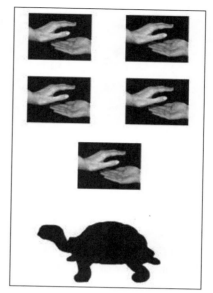

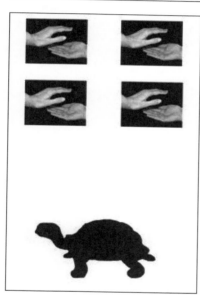

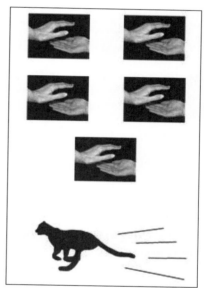

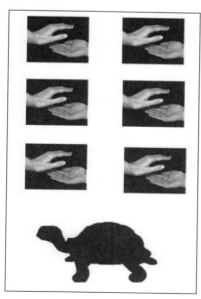

Bingo call cards

1.5 Recall
See, Imagine, Memorise

In my experience many adult learners with learning disabilities struggle to imagine abstract concepts such as future possibilities or other people's internal states. Our imaginations are vital to learning, from planning and organising ideas to retaining and recalling information. This fun activity can help students practise using basic imagination techniques to build 'mind pictures' as a tool to help recall.

Aims

- Create the opportunity for participation and turn taking.

- Develop awareness of others.

- Create the opportunity to learn a simple memory aid – basic imaginative links.

- Practise verbal labels for everyday objects.

Resources (for eight students)

You may have fewer than eight students in the group, in which case only use as many of these objects as you have students.

- 8 empty containers of the same variety (shoe boxes/gift boxes/pillow cases/silver take-away food containers with lids/empty ice cream tubs).

- 8 household objects (e.g. CD, fork, toothbrush, ball of string, clothes peg, pencil, sticky tape, camera, paintbrush, cup, remote control, pen, spectacles). (Actual objects provide an added sensory layer and enable a stronger visualisation, but if time is short to collect them you will need to print off a picture of each item and pass them round with an envelope for each student.)

- Pens and sheets for Differentiation and development, if required.

Prior to the activity

- Print off the two picture sheets (you will need two copies for each student as the activity will be performed twice).

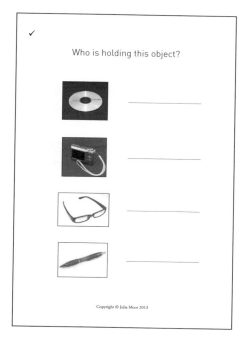

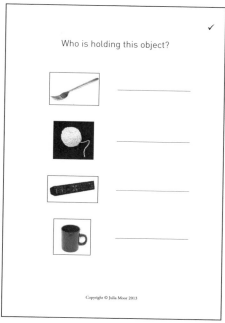

- Gather together actual items (or print off photos and collect envelopes) and containers.

Delivering the activity

Begin by discussing memory – do students forget things? Do they wish they had better memories? Who can remember the very first person they saw today? Or, what colour socks are they wearing? Perhaps talk about a time when you forgot something important yourself, for example where you parked the car!

Discuss how the key to trying to remember things is imagination – being able to see things in your mind. As a warm up to the activity try asking students to imagine their favourite meal. How does it smell? What does it look like? Where would they normally eat it? At what time of day? Get your students 'visualising'. Go on to explain to your students that you will be practising 'visualising' to help them remember things.

Show students the collection of containers (or envelopes with pictures) and explain that in each one there is an everyday object for them to take a look at and describe to the group. Place the containers in the middle of the table (or pass them around the group) and ask each student to take one, open it and see what's inside, then replace the lid.

Explain to the group that they will be trying to remember who has which item. Now go round the table once asking everyone to take out their object and say loudly what they have, one at a time, and then replace the object back in the box.

Hand out a copy of the picture sheet to each student and ask them to mark next to each object which person they think is holding it. There are several ways to do this:

- You may want to write a list of student names, copy it and hand each player a set for them to select, cut out and stick.

- Some, or all, of your students may be able to write independently or copy independently the name of the student from a pre-typed list.

- For students unable to do either of these, provide a set of photographs of the group – it is always useful to have a photo of each student from the start of the course (following consent). The student then selects and glues the photo in place.

Compare results – did everyone get this right or was it difficult? Was it easier to remember what was in your own box?

Now explain that you are going to help the group work on a simple memory aid. Ask everyone to re-select a different object and as you go around each player, ask them to find an imaginative way to link that person with the object. For example, Susan may select the cup. Now imagine Susan at a sink washing the biggest pile of cups imaginable. Get the group to contribute to the imagery. How long does it take her to wash the cups? How does she feel? David may select the peg. Ask the group to imagine David with a peg on his nose. Remind the group to make the links as imaginative as possible. Go round every student and make a link as a group, taking in suggestions for links and settling on the wildest, most imaginative ones. Now ask the group to repeat the exercise. Did they find that exercise easier? Your students should have been able to remember better this time.

Go on to ask your students if they can think of everyday situations where this type of memory aid may help them.

Some examples may be:

- Remembering to return an item to someone.

- Remembering to phone someone.

- Remembering someone's job or interests.

Differentiation and development

- For students with fine motor skills difficulties, stop sheets from sliding around by securing them to the table with masking tape. To assist the student to stick the written label or student photo to the sheet, place two-sided tape already in place on the sheet or use sticky tack rather than glue.

- This activity can work well for learners with visual impairments, provided items are described out loud at the start of the exercise so that the learner can make a strong link between the voice/name and the object (which can be handled and felt).

- Students working on literacy may use the alternative sheet with written labels.

✓

Who is holding this object?

Camera   _____

Spectacles   _____

Pen   _____

Remote
control   _____

Fork   _____

String   _____

Cup   _____

CD   _____

- Students with severe communication challenges may wish to match pictures to actual objects as a separate activity.

You may wish to use the resources for further activities as follows:

- **Memory**: Arrange some of objects on a tray in the centre of the table and time the students for three minutes to look at them. Now cover them up or remove them and ask students to write down as many items as they can remember. Learners could work in pairs or small groups with some talking, and some writing (i.e. working together as a team).

- **Spoken communication development**: Students could choose a box with an object in it, take a peep inside and then allow each member of the group to ask one question from the suggested list before taking a guess.

Who is holding this object?

_____

_____

_____

_____

Who is holding this object?

_____

_____

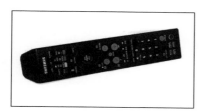

_____

_____

✓

Who is holding this object?

Camera _____

Spectacles _____

Pen _____

Remote
control _____

Fork _____

String _____

Cup _____

CD _____

Ask a question...

1. Will it fit inside a toilet roll tube?

2. Is it found in the kitchen?

3. Is it made of plastic?

4. Is it made of metal?

5. Can it be used to send a parcel?

6. Can it be used as a container?

7. Does it need a battery to work?

8. Does it hold things together?

1.6 Recall
A Group Picture Study

This visual memory activity works well as an extension to the previous session (Activity 1.5) and is designed to help focus students' attention on visual memory and recall with several layers of differentiation for a variety of abilities. Remember to make full use of all the learning and communication opportunities that the images inspire. I find the beach scene often invokes pleasant memories and sensory language, and creates many opportunities for students to share thoughts and ideas.

Aims

- Create opportunity for participation.

- Develop concentration on visual information.

- Practise and focus attention on visual recall.

- Practise fine motor skills.

Resources

- A copy of the blank beach scene, a complete beach scene and the individual elements for each student.

- Print off resources for differentiation.

- Sticky tack.

- A timer.

- CD player (optional).

- Laminator.
    (If you wish to use the activity several times, laminate the pictures and separate images for durability. If you are running short on printer ink, there is a line drawing version!)

Prior to the activity

Gather and print resources (including the differentiated ones detailed below) and laminate blank scenes and individual elements sheets depending on how durable you wish the activity to be.

Delivering the activity

Start the session by talking about how we don't always 'see' when we 'look', for example we don't always notice or take in what we are seeing from day to day. Does anyone know what the colour of the door was that they walked through? Ask students to close their eyes and describe the clothes that the person next to them is wearing. Discuss why it is useful to try to make a mental note of what we see around us as we go through the day. Make sure the following are included:

Being aware of our surroundings means…

- We feel in control and less 'lost' when out and about.

- We are more likely to notice if something is wrong or missing.

- We are more likely to dress appropriately for the weather and situation.

- We are less likely to lose our things if we really 'see' where we put them.

- We are more likely to cope in an emergency if we know where, for example, the fire exits are or the phone is.

Learning often involves visual information; learning to really 'see' what is in front of us will help us to learn.

Students will also offer their own equally valid individual suggestions.

Describe how the following activity will help to 'exercise' our eyes and brains to assist us to remember what we have seen.

Let everyone study the beach scene picture for five minutes. It may help students to concentrate by playing some music quietly in the background during this time – beach/sea sounds will add to the activity as a multi-sensory experience.

After five minutes, collect the pictures back in and hand out a copy of the empty scene. Allow students time to take in the image and share their own thoughts and ideas about the scene… How does it look compared to the busy version? Lonely? Calm?

Can students recall what is missing? Allow several minutes for students to come up with ideas for the missing elements. Now hand everyone a set of the separate images.

Ask the students to cut out (or present pre-cut images to those who may find this too difficult) and position these as accurately as possible on the photo to match the one they have studied. Depending on the ability of the group, you may wish to give students a timed set of minutes to complete the activity, and space seating well so that they are not swayed by others' choices!

Differentiation and development

- For students with difficulties manipulating the smaller images, glue these onto thick card and secure the blank image to the table with masking tape.

- For students who are finding the activity too difficult, use the 'jigsaw version' as the spaces offer more clues to position in this variation.

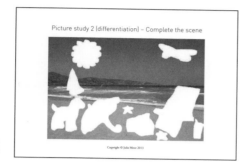

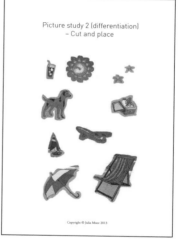

- Students still struggling? Take a copy of the beach picture and cut it into four or eight equal pieces. Task the student to piece/stick these together 'jigsaw style' to make the whole scene again.

- For students working on literacy, provide a copy of the blank scene, and ask students to either cut or paste the word label or write the word label on the blank scene.

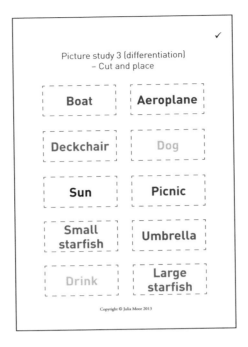

- Art/creativity groups may wish to use the line drawing version of the above:

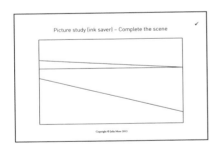  

- Images can be traced/applied freehand or coloured and pasted. You may also wish to use this version if you have a large group to save on printer ink!

- Your students may wish to make their own version of this activity using their images (scene photos/pictures torn from magazines). Ask students to draw some separate items to add to the scene on a spare piece of A4. Suggestions are animals/cars/clouds/trees, and so on. Alternatively provide stencils or pre-cut shapes to colour.

- Students arrange the images onto scenes using sticky tack – working in twos means students can set the layout for each other. Photocopy the complete scene then remove the images and repeat the activity as described above.

Additional resources for this development activity

- A set of printed 'scenes', postcards or magazines with scenic views (beach scenes work well as students can add deckchairs, boats, dogs, birds, etc.).

- Felt pens, stencils.

- White card.

- Scissors.

- Sticky tack.

- Access to photocopier.

You may wish to make your own different sets of the activity according to seasons, holidays or topic themes using Google images, clip art or students' own photos. Starting a session with an activity like this motivates students to engage with something highly visual which makes less demands on verbal instructions. It gets students thinking about and using language around a particular theme and sets the scene for participation in learning through 'doing'.

Creative writing groups may develop the activity further by using the scene to create a storyline.

Activity 1.7 supports this activity as a natural development to giving and receiving instructions using 'place' words.

Picture study – Complete the scene

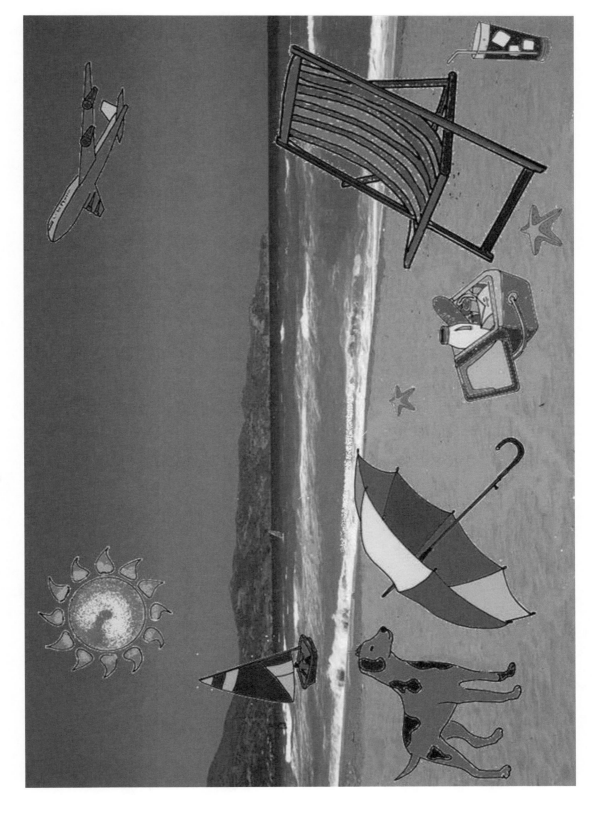

Picture study – Cut and place

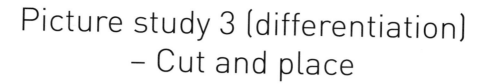

Picture study 3 (differentiation) – Cut and place

Boat	**Aeroplane**
Deckchair	**Dog**
Sun	**Picnic**
Small starfish	**Umbrella**
Drink	**Large starfish**

Picture study (ink saver) – Complete the scene

Picture study (ink saver) – Look and remember

Picture study (ink saver)
– Cut and place

1.7 Recall
Picture Prepositions

Common barriers many of my students face when trying to keep on task are difficulties in listening to and interpreting instructions. Practice in giving and following verbal instructions helps remind learners to really listen and practise holding parts of language in memory long enough to act on them. This activity is designed to help focus students' attention on listening, processing and acting on instructions using positional language. Although this is good practice for students already competent in interpreting positional language, including left and right, the main benefit of the activity is developing and practising the memory and concentration skills to both give and carry out an instruction accurately.

Aims

- Develop concentration on listening.

- Develop skills at receiving and processing instructions.

- Develop skills at giving clear instructions.

- Create opportunity for participation.

- Review and assess language processing for 'place' words.

Resources

- A copy of the picture sheets for each student, either pasted onto card or laminated.

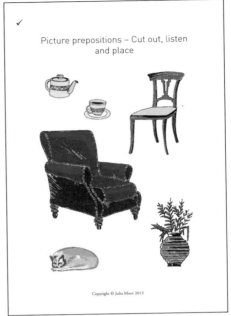

- Several copies of the 'scene' sheet cut into their separate scenes (one scene per student).

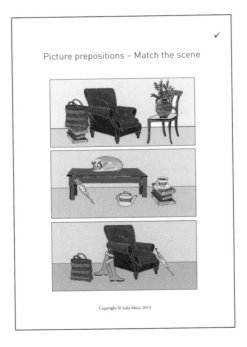

- Sticky tack.

- A small empty box and a coin.

- Blank A4 cards – either plain card or laminated plain A4 paper (one for each student).

- Several copies of the cue sheet.

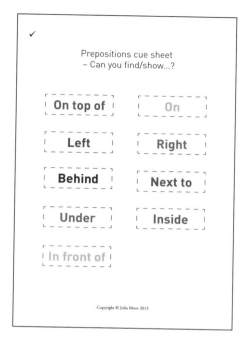

Prepositions cue sheet
– Can you find/show...?

On top of   On

Left   Right

Behind   Next to

Under   Inside

In front of

Copyright © Julia Moor 2013

- Shallow box or card to make a screen.

Prior to the activity

Gather resources and print off picture sheets, laminate (or paste onto card) and cut out individual picture items.

Delivering the activity

Commence the activity by discussing instructions. Do students have difficulties remembering or following instructions on where to locate things or giving directions? For example, if someone asks 'Collect the key from the envelope under the pile of books on the left hand table in the hall', can students visualise where this is and remember the instruction or would they have problems retaining this complex instruction? Make a quick assessment of abilities by talking about 'place' words. Ask students for examples of place words (in/on/under/next to/opposite); can they demonstrate with the box and the coin?

Provide each learner with a set of laminated/cut out images and a blank sheet of A4 card. Check all students know the verbal labels for the images. Demonstrate how to give a clear verbal instruction, for example, 'put the cat UNDER the table', 'put the book ON the chair', 'put the lamp ON the table'. Support students to not be influenced by others' interpretation by working inside a shallow box or behind a makeshift screen made from card.

Now ask for volunteers, one at a time, to give an instruction to the group for where to place several images (onto the blank card) in relation to each other (with sticky tack). After each instruction, ask students to lift their picture up to compare with each other and the 'instruction giver' where they have placed their image. Keep the activity fun and engaging in a variety of ways:

- Make up a fictional dialogue about the scene. For example, 'Forgetful Sue has lost her blue shopping bag. She's in the kitchen shouting through to her friend Kate in the living room. "It's next to your boots," shouts Kate…'

- Try following the instructions yourself with your own set of images. Turn some upside down or on their side and remind learners that we make assumptions about how things will look, for example the teapot will be upright without having to say it's upright.

You may want to try splitting the group into pairs, where one student *gives* the instruction verbally by following a 'scene' card, for example 'put the teapot under the table', and the other *receives* and carries out the instruction on their card. Provide a screen for the students to work behind – this could be a box on its side or a large piece of card taped to the table. After several instructions, compare results by moving the screen.

Differentiation and development

For students with fine motor skills difficulties you may want to try attaching hook and loop strips to the back of the images and across a plain scene card.

- For students with visual difficulties try setting up a 3D version of the activity using two each of the following: cup, straw, ruler, spoon, book, key – any collection of household objects that you can get two of and set up the activity with a screen as described for 'givers and receivers'.

- The activity can be scaled down for students with speech difficulties by copying the scene directly.

- You may wish to develop the activity further by building into sessions a time for following real instructions, for example, 'return the rulers to the box under the bottom shelf'. Ask students: what would help them locate things in the home better? Ideas may include picture labels/colour codes, see-through containers, having less things to organise, multi-purpose items, or adding tactile or auditory markers to items. For example, 'all blue' clothing could have a ribbon on the hanger and 'all black' clothing could have a small pet bell to assist visually impaired students to identify and put together outfits.

Picture prepositions – Cut out, listen and place

Picture prepositions – Cut out, listen and place

Picture prepositions – Match the scene

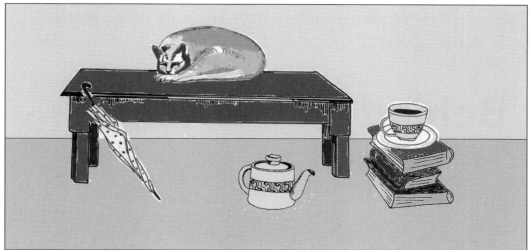

Prepositions cue sheet
– Can you find/show...?

On top of	On
Left	Right
Behind	Next to
Under	Inside
In front of	

1.8 Senses
A Sensory Composition

Adult learners usually enjoy the opportunity to be creative, with lots of visual content and tactile resources. This activity will maximise the potential for students to engage with a variety of media. The photography element gives learners the opportunity to come away with an effective and professional looking piece of work to motivate students to engage with the task.

Aims

- Create an opportunity to choose/reach out/explore/arrange/manipulate.

- Create an opportunity to discuss textures, colours and patterns.

- Create an opportunity to evaluate own and others' creative work.

- Create an opportunity to produce and develop a finished piece of creative work.

- Create an opportunity to work as a pair/negotiate/cooperate.

Resources

- A collection of fabrics and papers in different colours and textures.

- Shells, beads, bells, pebbles, marbles, fir cones, cotton reels, artificial flowers, pipe cleaners, pom-poms, buttons – anything decorative that can be incorporated into a photo. (Remember these items can then be returned to the art room for further use – so although the activity requires access to a range of resources, it can be repeated many times with several groups of students, eventually recycling the materials for other projects. Students may like to bring in their own special objects to be used in the work: jewellery, postcards, small ornaments.)

- A set of deep trays (one for each pair of students); new cat litter trays are ideal.

- • Digital camera and tripod stand/laptop and printer.

- • Papers or fabrics to create backgrounds (black paper works well to absorb light and reduce flash glare).

Prior to the activity

Gather together your resources and print some example photos of your own or the example collection on the CD (preferably in colour) to assist in communicating to students what they will be making.

Delivering the activity

Start the activity by handing round the sample picture to explain what you will be trying to achieve. Ask if anyone has used a digital camera before and assess how much one-to-one support individuals will require. Explain that anyone can do this and achieve good results. Make it clear that although the items are to touch and arrange, there is no 'sticking' and no wet textures to touch (this can be a negative aspect of artwork for some students). Group students into working pairs and hand round the trays of objects to create a discussion point such as favourite colours/

textures/patterns. After everyone has seen and touched the tray contents ask them to select a collection of objects that they like the look and/or feel of, including a fabric or paper to form the tray background. They will have to agree with their partner about their choices which may mean making compromises and negotiations.

When each pair has a pile of items, empty the trays and give one tray to each partnership.

Allow plenty of time for the students to arrange the items in the tray. They may want to 'make a picture' or arrange them in an abstract way. They may wish to manipulate the materials, for example, twist/scrunch/thread. Ask if their partners agree with the arrangements – maybe they want to take turns to make their own design rather than a joint one. The trays enable students who may take a while to set up their work a means to contain the arrangement over more than one session if required. The trays also contain small objects which reduces the frustration of things rolling off the table or getting nudged by others as they work. When a tray is 'arranged', support students to set up the camera and demonstrate how to take a picture; take several, some zoom shots, some wide shots. If you have a camera that allows you, try some in black and white/sepia.

If time/facilities allow, it works well to have a laptop and printer set up for students to look at their work – ideally a projector for a whole group discussion!

Encourage all students to make choices about which version of their photo they want to see in print. Once the photos are printed off on glossy paper and handed round, can the students find their own photos? Discuss which pictures *they* like and why. If resources don't allow this, then black and white copies on a smaller scale will still work.

Differentiation and development

- Be mindful of the materials available for students with fine motor skills problems and keep items large enough to manipulate.

- If students are unable to operate the shutter button on the camera, still encourage them to direct the shot by looking at the image display and deciding on the best position. Encourage all students to make choices about which version of their photo they want to see in print.

- Students with visual impairments can get very much involved in choosing, feeling and arranging the items on their composition. It may assist these students to attach items using tack or two sided tape so that they don't disturb the arrangement as they work. These students may also want to make a tactile landscape using the actual objects (on card or ply) to keep.

- For pre-verbal students, remember to demonstrate every step in stages.

- For students struggling to make the choices to arrange the materials, limit to three items and set up an arrangement to copy.

- For students working on early literacy, the work can be developed further by mounting the photo onto card and then writing descriptive words around the outside of the mount, or for those developing IT skills, they can type the words onto the photo in a photo editing program.

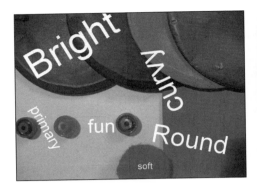 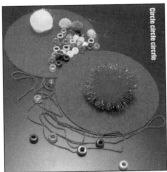 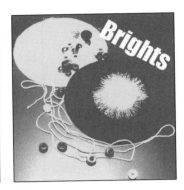

- If students have access to laptops and an editing program, then they can get really creative experimenting with visual effects, from increasing colour saturation to making pencil drawings of their photos to then colour by hand.

 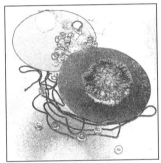 

- Discuss how the photos can be used. Maybe they can be made into calendars, or printed onto fabric transfer to put on a cushion or apron. They could be made into photo greetings cards or perhaps several could be mounted together as a collage.

- Good presentation will create artwork that students can really feel proud to display. Bring in a selection of light card mounts (pre-prepare at home using a knife/cutting mat) and let the students choose which displays their artwork the best.

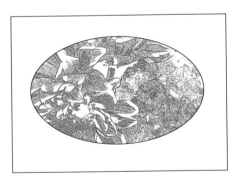  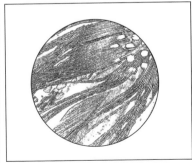

SECTION 2

Cooperation and Teamwork

Introduction

Activity 2.1 Manners Bingo

Activity 2.2 Hands on the Line

Activity 2.3 Act it Out

Activity 2.4 Board Game Builder

Activity 2.5 A Flock of Poems

Activity 2.6 Meal Maker

Activity 2.7 Collage Race

Activity 2.8 Team Art

 All photocopiable sheets that accompany these activities can also be printed in colour from the CD at the back of the book. This icon denotes any sheets that can be found on the CD, but are not included in this book.

Introduction

Students with communication disabilities often restrict their communication attempts to teaching and support staff – people who they feel will bridge verbal language barriers and make allowances based on previous experience or interactions. Staff may automatically adjust conversation to include favoured subjects, strip language down and adjust their volume and body language to give the student the best possible chance to understand the interaction. Many peers within groups tend not to do this between themselves, focusing instead on making themselves heard as individuals; I am often fielding several conversations at once on a one-to-one basis, changing and adjusting my vocabulary and delivery as I go. By feeding into the course, small group activities students get to know and appreciate each other in a controlled and supported environment, which develops confidence in interacting with peers and is a baseline from which to work on skills such as cooperation and compromise. Once again, success depends on how motivating the activity is and this means getting the pitch right with rigorous differentiation. It also means keeping things highly visual to give students the tools they need to engage with each other.

Many of the activities within the whole book include opportunities for students to engage with each other and ways for session leaders to scaffold those interactions. The following eight activities specifically require students to work with each other to achieve a result, each making a unique contribution through their role, or task, or by holding a key resource, or demonstrating a personal skill.

2.1 Manners Bingo

This activity is designed to start a discussion about acceptable and appropriate behaviour within a group learning environment. I find that if I have one student needing support in this area that to tackle this as a group enables the individual to be more aware of monitoring their own behaviour without the need to isolate them as 'challenging' or 'attention seeking'. The game creates a neutral context to facilitate group discussion, allowing individuals to identify their own support needs to settle into a social learning environment.

This would be a useful activity at the start of a course of sessions to enable learners to set their own boundaries and remind them about common good manners when working within a group. I find students enjoy working out what the pictures represent and creating one sentence statements about each 'code' of politeness.

Aims

- Create the opportunity to focus attention on positive social behaviour.

- Create an opportunity to discuss own expectations of good manners within a group.

- Develop skills at identifying own areas for behaviour development in a learning context.

- Create an opportunity for early numeracy work – symbol/label recognition.

- Create an opportunity to participate in a group activity.

- Develop skills at decoding picture representations.

Resources

- A bingo playing card for each student (there are 8 available; to create extras you can print/copy/mix and match images).

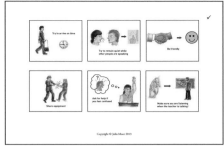

- 2 sets of 'Bingo call cards' – a 'picture only' set and a set with the 'manners rule' written on them.

- A set of either plastic numbers or large cards with numbers printed on them.

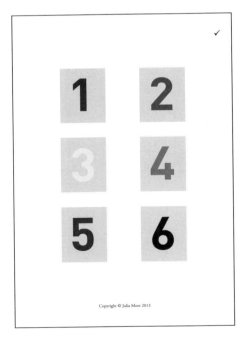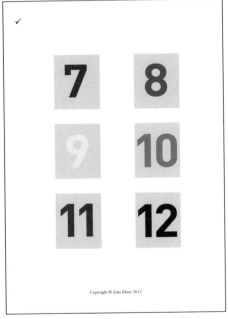

- Counters – these can be anything you have to hand in multiples. I tend to collect the plastic tops off milk cartons for this purpose as you will need 48 counters for a group of eight students. You can also cut coloured card into squares to use as counters too.

Prior to the activity

- Gather the resources.

- Print off and laminate/paste onto card the bingo playing cards.

- Print off and laminate/paste onto card the bingo call cards and number the back of the 'picture only' cards 1–12 with a thick marker pen.

- Print off and laminate/paste onto card the numbers.

- Collect a small box/container for students to draw the number out of.

Delivering the activity

Begin a dialogue about good manners when working in a group. Which behaviours do students like/dislike in others? Offer some ideas if suggestions are reluctant. For example, do students like or dislike others talking when they are trying to talk? Do they like or dislike being greeted verbally/with a handshake? Do they like doors being held open? People sharing equipment? Picking bags off the floor? Encourage all students to respond to the discussion with a vote. Look at the general lines of agreement. Does everyone agree that there are certain bad manners that everyone dislikes and certain good manners that everyone likes? Encourage lots of examples. Are there any manners that students know they struggle to regulate, for example jumping into conversations before they forget their point? Explain that to help the group work together with the best manners possible you will be using some picture symbols throughout the course but that you will need everyone to be clear about what they mean. One at a time introduce the 'picture only' call cards to the students. What do students think the pictures represent? Can they create a one sentence statement such as, 'Greet each other with a friendly smile', or 'Share equipment sensibly'. Compare the student suggestions for the 'picture only' call cards to their matching cards with the manners rule written on.

Ask students to choose a bingo playing card and six counters each.

Proceed to play the bingo game by asking students one at a time to select a number (put these in a box to pass around). This is a good initial assessment for number recognition/matching. As bingo caller, ask volunteers to match the number to the number written on the back of the 'picture only' call card and hold it up or pass it round for the group to examine. Who has a matching image and manners rule on their cards? The first student to place counters on all six of their images is declared the winner.

Differentiation and development

- If students aren't working on numeracy or struggle to use a selection method with numbers, then simply place the picture call cards in the box or ask students to find the matching colour of the number instead.

- For students working on early literacy, use the bingo cards with written statements only on them.

		✓
Try to arrive on time	Try to remain quiet while other people are speaking	Be friendly
Make sure you are listening when the teacher is talking!	Share equipment	Ask for help if you feel confused

- Visually impaired students who are Braille users would be easily able to access the game with a Braille card if you have access to a Braille embosser. Make sure they have a means to secure their counters to the card using hook and loop dots.

- The call cards can become prompt cards to be used in further sessions to assist students to regulate behaviours that may become disruptive to learning. Pictures could be displayed on the classroom walls for a teacher to point to or kept as a moveable set of cue cards. They can be used discreetly by the teacher or teaching assistant to remind a student without drawing attention to them or stopping a line of thought.

- Students could develop and contribute their own ideas about what constitutes politeness within the classroom. There may be something specific to the environment they find themselves in or the type of class.

- The 'bingo' game format can be used to familiarise students with everything from the names of others in the group to course-specific equipment, language and resources. It can also be used to revise and review previous learning. Ask each student to make one bingo card making sure that at least two items are different between cards. Students can then either keep or swap cards and play as a group.

Note: It may be that several players are waiting for the same three pictures. Remind students that the first to say bingo or hold up their card is the winner, to keep the game competitive.

Keep coats and bags off the floor

No shouting!

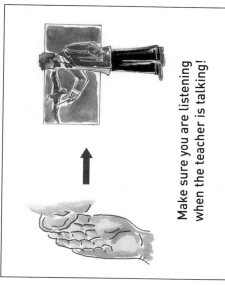

Make sure you are listening when the teacher is talking!

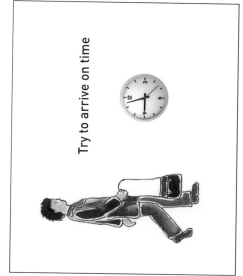

Try to arrive on time

Switch off mobiles please!

Ask for help if you feel confused

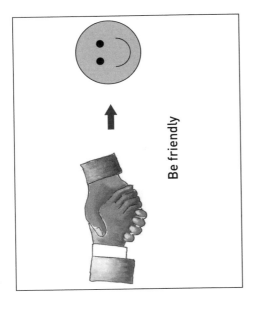

Be friendly

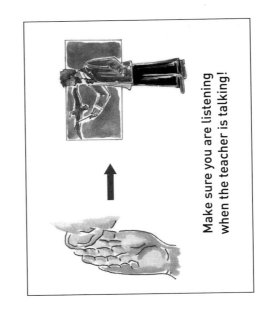

Make sure you are listening when the teacher is talking!

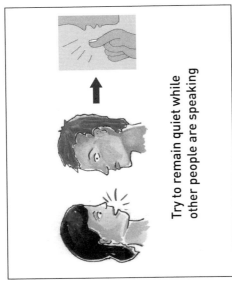

Try to remain quiet while other people are speaking

Ask for help if you feel confused

Try to arrive on time

Share equipment

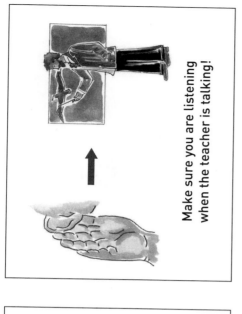

Make sure you are listening when the teacher is talking!

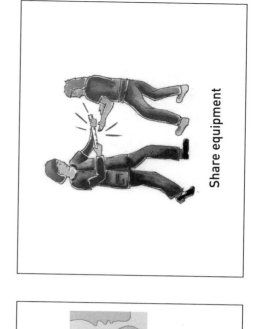

Share equipment

Share ideas

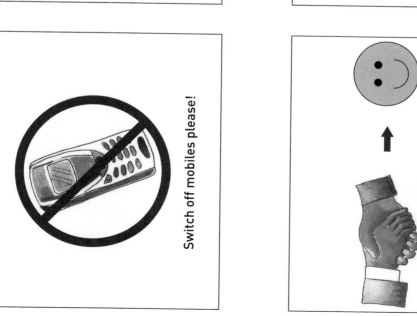

Try to remain quiet while other people are speaking

Switch off mobiles please!

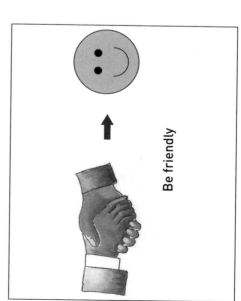

Be friendly

Ask for help if
you feel confused

No shouting!

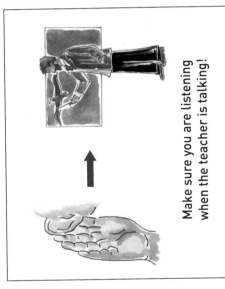

Make sure you are listening
when the teacher is talking!

Try to remain quiet while
other people are speaking

Switch off mobiles please!

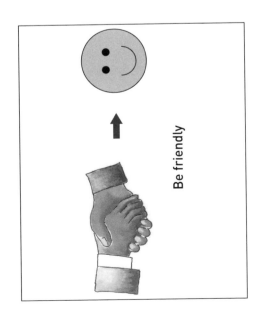

Be friendly

Copyright © Julia Moor 2013

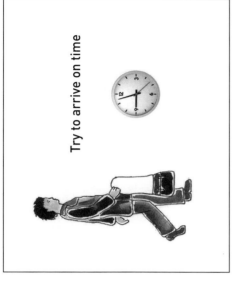

Try to arrive on time

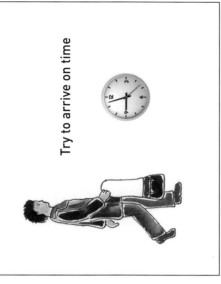

Ask for help if
you feel confused

Share ideas

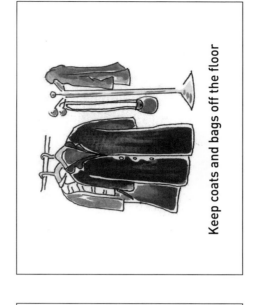

Keep coats and bags off the floor

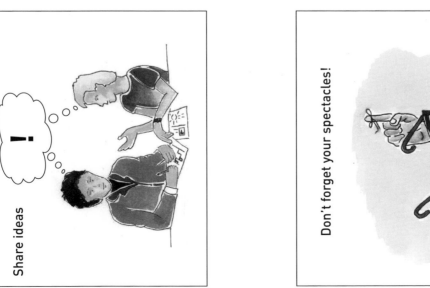

Please use a hankerchief
for coughs and sneezes

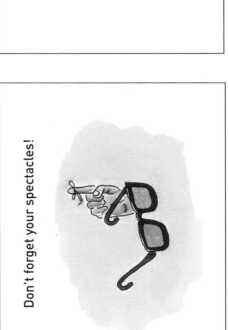

Don't forget your spectacles!

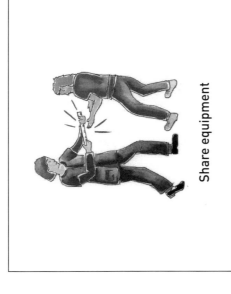

Share equipment

Ask for help if you feel confused

Share ideas

Keep coats and bags off the floor

Switch off mobiles please!

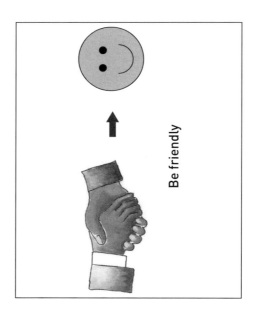

Be friendly

Try to arrive on time

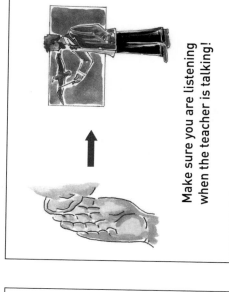

Make sure you are listening when the teacher is talking!

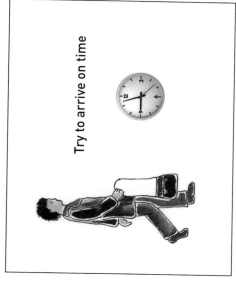

Share ideas

No shouting

Switch off mobiles please!

Don't forget your spectacles!

Please use a hankerchief for coughs and sneezes

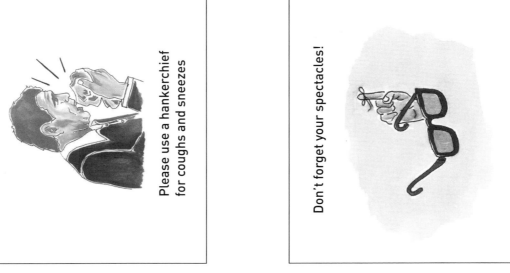

Don't forget your spectacles!

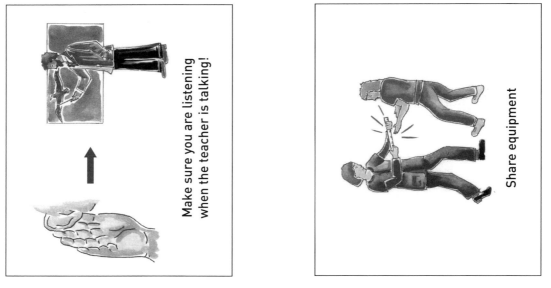

Make sure you are listening when the teacher is talking!

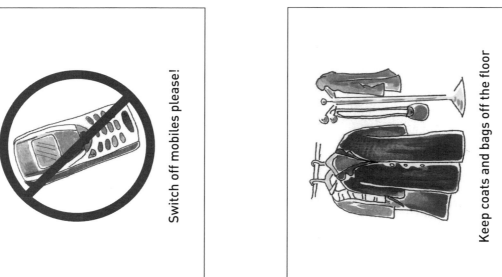

Share equipment

Switch off mobiles please!

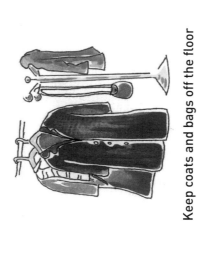

Keep coats and bags off the floor

Bingo call cards (no words)

  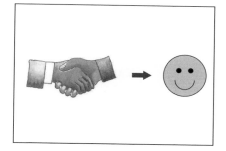

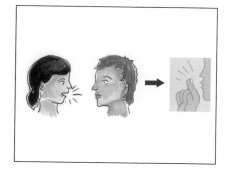  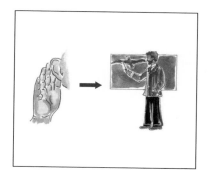

Bingo call cards (with words)

No shouting!

Please use a hankerchief for coughs and sneezes

Switch off mobiles please!

Share ideas

Ask for help if you feel confused

Share equipment

Don't forget your spectacles!

Try to arrive on time

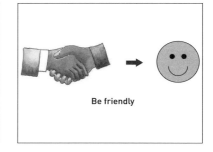

Be friendly

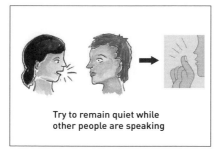

Try to remain quiet while other people are speaking

Keep coats and bags off the floor

Make sure you are listening when the teacher is talking!

✓

7

8

9

10

11

12

Try to arrive
on time

Try to remain quiet
while other people
are speaking

Be friendly

Make sure you
are listening
when the teacher
is talking!

Share equipment

Ask for help
if you feel
confused

2.2 Hands on the Line

This physical activity motivates students to make eye contact, encourages tracking an object in and out of other people's hands, physically brings students into closer proximity and draws in those that may otherwise migrate to the periphery. There are several ways and cognitive levels to play this game with the basic premise being to pass an object or picture card that has been threaded onto a plastic line amongst students. The line is a symbolic and physical bond that creates a sense of belonging to a group and enables students to see themselves as an integral part of a team. It's also a physical aid to those that need it and creates many opportunities to assist and work together to move the items along.

Aims

- Develop awareness of other members of the group.

- Develop imagination and vocabulary.

- Develop skills at observation and interpretation.

- Create the opportunity to cooperate with others on a task.

- Develop skills at finding semantic links between objects.

Resources

- A plastic washing line big enough to form a loose ring that all students can hold and allows a comfortable space between players.

- A CD player and choice of music; this adds an extra sense dimension to the activity and cues players to 'pass till the music stops'.

- A single hole punch.

- A4 cards or recycle used greetings cards.

- Narrow ribbon/string/food ties.

- A set of pictures or objects depending on which activity you choose below.

Prior to the activity

- Print out the sets of matching pictures:

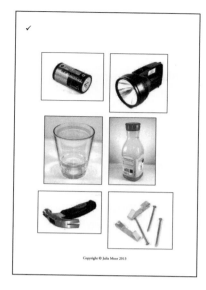

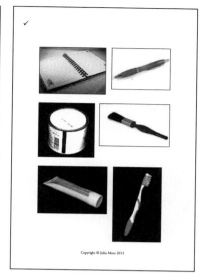

- Fold the card in half or fold used greeting cards inside out (so the front cover is blank) and attach a picture on the inside (over the existing printed picture if recycling greetings cards).

- Punch a hole in the top corner so that the string can pass through the card to tie it onto the line.

Delivering the activity

Explain that we can see partnerships in all areas of daily living, this includes people too. Some people may be great at something such as the mechanics of writing but not have the imaginative ideas, and someone else could have lots of ideas but be poor at spelling – they could pair up and make great work!

Discuss natural pairs, things that work better/look better/are more useful when they have each other, for example dustpan and brush, cup and saucer, lamp and bulb, vase and flowers.

Tie all the cards onto the line (you may wish to start with a small number of pairs, for example four pairs/eight cards, until the group get the hang of it).

Ask learners to arrange their seating in a loose oval shape and spread the line out so everyone is able to hold a portion of the string. Pass the cards around the group on the string to music.

When the music stops each player holds onto the card they have and opens it up to look at it (without sharing its contents with the group).

The first person to take a turn will be identified by the session leader (or be a volunteer) and they will have one guess at who has their matching card. For example, they may have opened a card with 'toothpaste' on it and guessed that Kate has a picture that it may go with (i.e. 'toothbrush'). Kate shows or tells the player what her picture is. If the player identifies that the two go together, then the matching picture is untied from the line and handed over. The music starts and the cards get passed again. If the two cards cannot be paired, then the players each take a guess around the ring until a pair is made and the music can start again. If no pairs are made, then once everyone has guessed in turn and the game is back to the original player, then the music starts again. When the music stops, the next person to guess will be the one sitting on the left of the first player, and so on in a clockwise direction. When all the cards have been untied and made into pairs, the player with the most pairs is the winner.

Differentiation and development

- For an *easier version* of the game, separate the pictures and their partners into two piles and ask students to choose a picture at random from one pile to keep hold of. From the second pile, thread one picture onto the line and pass to music. When the music stops the person holding it will take a look and decide if it goes with their own or not. If it does, untie and keep and the session leader threads another picture. If not, then keep going until it lands on its partner.

- *Even easier…* If students struggle to identify semantic partners, then print two sets of identical picture cards and play as a matching activity.

- For students *developing vocabulary*, instead of guessing the person holding the matching card, players can make a guess at what the matching picture might be and ask the group, 'Who has the…' For example, a student looking at a photo of a plant may ask the group for 'sunshine'. The matching photo for this is a 'watering can'; students will have to try to remember items that the others have asked for in order to work out what they could ask for. The person holding the 'watering can' may originally think to ask for 'tap' but may change this to 'plant' when they have heard the first request. If a student asks for a match and someone has it then they hand it over, or no one may have it as it could still be 'hanging on the line'. When everyone has 'asked', the round starts again, and is repeated until all the cards have gone.

- The game can be adapted for students with *visual impairments* as follows: Place a set of picture cards in a box and tie a set of matching real objects to the line. Suggestions are: peg, key, paperclip, sock, torch, bracelet, watch, scarf. Ask a sighted student to select a picture card and tell the group what it is. Now pass the objects round to music and when the music stops, the player with the real object which matches the picture unties and keeps it.

- Or simply pass objects until the music stops and ask either each student one by one or a named student, to either feel and identify their object, or describe it to the group for the group to guess.

Variation

For students needing encouragement to cooperate, remember names or get to know each other, randomly hand a card to each student that goes with an object or picture tied to the line. Pass objects/pictures along the line and when the music stops everyone removes the object or card off the line. The players then have ten minutes to talk to each other and trade cards and objects until everyone has a matching pair.

Finally, for a 'poker face' version to complement work on facial expression, assign each student a number. Pass just one item that can easily be held and concealed in the hand, for example a key, and when the music stops, select a number at random and this student has to guess who is hiding the key. Remind students not to give away their secret through facial expression. If you are playing with six or fewer students you could use a dice to select who guesses (or add two dice faces for 12 or fewer students).

You could use the principle of this activity to make a tailor-made version to help students familiarise themselves with resources specific to a course. For example, a money management course may use pictures of coins and match them to a written value/each other/the real coin, depending on ability level. Literacy students could pass adjectives and match them to photos, for example cold/ice, furry/dog, spiky/cactus.

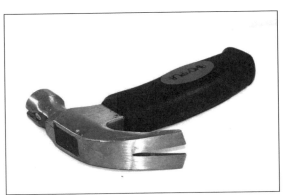

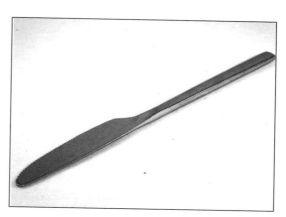

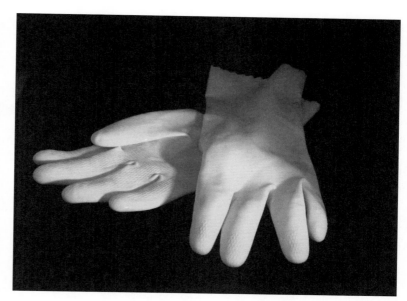

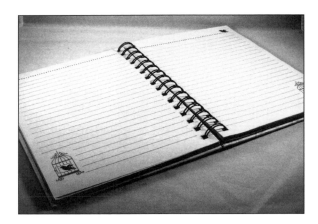

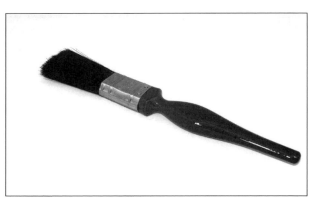

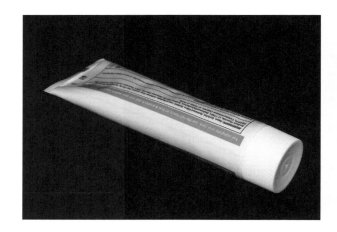

2.3 Act it Out

In this role-playing activity, students are acting in pairs; they will feel less self-conscious and more likely to engage than they would during individual role play. The suggested 'roles' are everyday meaningful activities (e.g. a trip to the hairdresser) and the 'how' of the activity is broken into stages using visual references. The pairs are decided on randomly. This prevents the same learners pairing up time and again and slowly builds up motivation to engage by starting with a simple, enjoyable selection process (passing cards around the group to music, 'pass the parcel' style). The activity uses lots of supportive visual cues, enabling learners to connect more readily with what they are being asked to mime.

Aims

- Create an opportunity to act out a situation.

- Develop skills in cooperating with a partner on a task.

- Develop imagination skills.

- Create an opportunity to take part in a group activity.

- Create the opportunity to discuss personal experience of the situations being acted.

- Create the opportunity to practise shape and colour matching.

Resources

- A set of 'role cards' (5 scenarios).

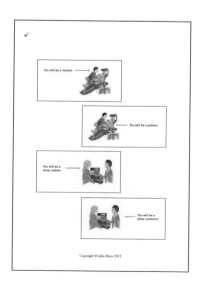

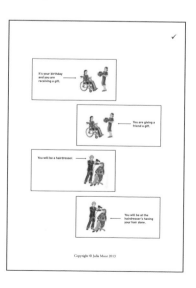

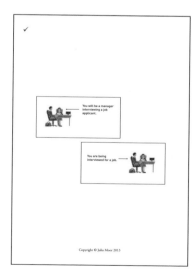

- A sheet of envelope shapes.

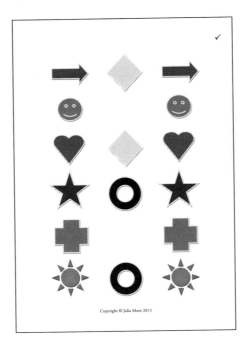

- A selection list for each student.

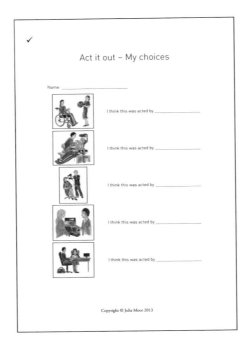

- A 'quiet' sign.

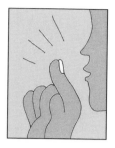

- A cue card for each acting pair.

- An envelope for each role card used (you could recycle used ones).

- CD player and a piece of music.

- An empty box/tray/bag – any container to hold the role cards to pass them around the group.

- Prints of the development materials as detailed below.

Prior to the activity

- Make sets of matching envelopes by cutting and sticking/taping a shape to the outside of each one.

- Print off resources including development sheets if this is suitable for your learners.

- Place the role cards inside the envelopes – make sure they are also paired into their matching roles.

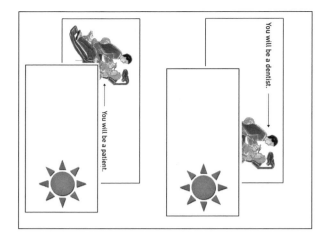

Delivering the activity

Discuss acting and role play with the group. Who enjoys performing, and who is more reticent? Support students who might react with a little anxiety about whether they will be supported. Explain that the activity is there to help learners think about rehearsing situations, predicting reactions and outcomes and making life seem a little more predictable. Tell the learners that to start off they will be acting out a set of everyday scenes in groups of two and they will need to work together to make the scene look convincing. They will spend some time discussing with their mime partner how they each will be feeling and behaving in the situation, what they will be doing and whether they will be using equipment or carrying items – all of these things will be mimed.

The first part of the activity is to select who works with whom and which mime they will be doing. This could just be decided by the session leader, though I find that a selection activity warms the group up to working with each other and cues them for group interaction and participation. Place all the matching envelopes in a container with a lid/a box or a bag, and pass this around the group to music (making sure that you have an envelope for each student, i.e. eight students/four pairs). If you have an odd number of students, then print a third matching card and ask that group to work as a three; for example, two clients/one hairdresser or dentist/patient and dental nurse. I find that my students enjoy this selection activity (which is reminiscent of 'pass the parcel'), they understand what is expected of them and this then motivates them to engage with the primary learning activity. The session leader stops the music (either with his or her back to the group for an arbitrary selection or facing the group if he or she would prefer certain learners to be together!). When the music stops, the student holding the box removes an envelope without opening it and the box is passed around and stopped again for a second student to remove the complementary role card. This becomes a simple 'matching same to same activity', enabling all students to feel successful and be 'part' of the group.

Ask the students not to open their envelopes just yet and repeat the activity for as many rounds as you need. When the box lands on a student who already has an envelope, they pass it on. Eventually everyone will be sat with a closed envelope marked with a shape.

Tell students they have five minutes to find the person in the group with the matching symbol on their envelope – that person will be their partner. If the environment allows, enable partners to sit next to each other, though this isn't necessary at this stage so long as they can identify who they are working with (by pointing/naming). This identification process again increases awareness of others in the group and can bring together students who might not normally interact with each other.

Describe how they will be acting out the picture on the card in the form of 'mime' and check that all students know that this means no talking. Show students the 'no talking' sign and explain that this will be held up to remind them if necessary.

Hand everyone a mime reminder cue card.

Go through an example mime not on the role cards, for example 'Meeting a long lost relative from the airport'. Use the mime reminder cue card and talk to the whole group:

- What would the person be feeling: angry/sad/happy/tired?

- Would they be moving fast or slow?

- Would they be carrying something?

- Would they be seated or standing?

- Would they be behaving very friendly and informal or just polite and formal?

- Would they be talking? How can we mime (i.e. say something without sound) talking?

Students can now open their envelopes and take a look at the mime card inside (without sharing it with the others). Now enable students to group into their pairs and move around the room to find their own space. Set a time limit of 10–15 minutes for rehearsal and walk around the group checking that students know what they are acting and how they will go about doing it.

Regroup the students and check that everyone is comfortable to 'perform' to the rest of the group (some may prefer to remain seated where they are). You could ask for volunteers to start or select groups by asking a learner to randomly choose one of the shapes used on the envelopes.

Be on hand to scaffold the mime – students may freeze, so support and enable learners to make actions by cueing verbally and non-verbally through gesture.

To assist the rest of the group to make a choice about what their peers are acting, they will have a visual selection list; this will narrow down choices and support imaginations. Students can write names on the lines or be given a set of student photos to glue next to the mime they have chosen.

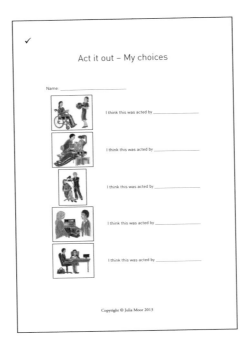

Differentiation and development

- For students who are finding this easy, leave out the above sheet and ask them to guess without the picture clues.

- If you feel the group needs extra clues then allow 'props'/clothing or phrases such as 'open wide' for the dentist.

- The activity is described above at its basic level; however for verbally confident students this could be developed to provide an opportunity to rehearse solutions to 'everyday social problems'. You could choose a 'scenario' to give to each pair (or write your own – there is a template on the CD).

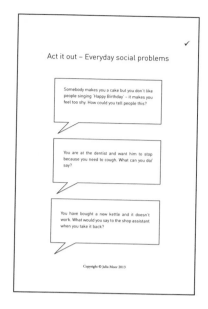
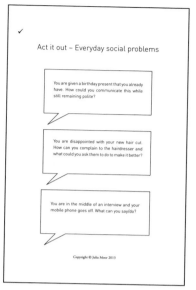

- You could also ask students to act out a scene using different feelings. For example, all students could act 'sunbathing', but then select a feeling to go with the mime, such as sleepy/happy/thoughtful/restless/sad/angry. The rest of the group can then choose the scenario and the feeling associated.

- You might also want to solicit from the group a real-life scenario that they would like to role play to help them in the future, for example 'asking a pharmacist for advice' or 'complaining about a service'.

✓

You will be a dentist. →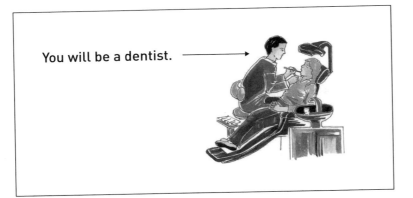

 ← You will be a patient.

You will be a shop cashier. →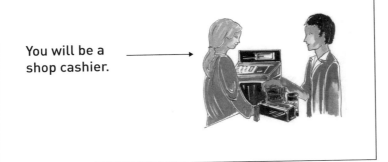

 ← You will be a shop customer.

It's your birthday and you are receiving a gift. →

← You are giving a friend a gift.

You will be a hairdresser. →

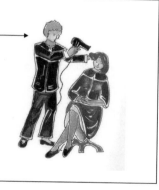

← You will be at the hairdresser's having your hair done.

 You will be a manager interviewing a job applicant.

You are being interviewed for a job.

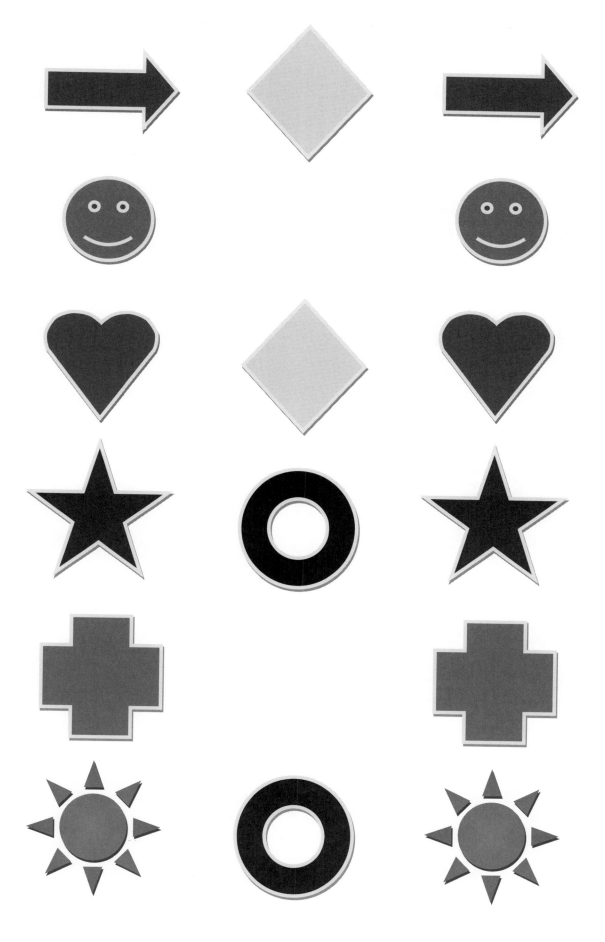

Act it out – My choices

Name: _____

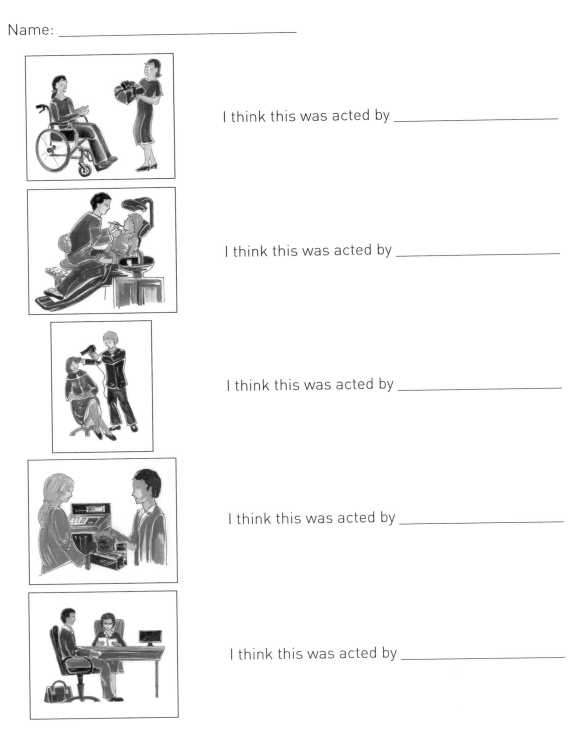

I think this was acted by _____

I think this was acted by _____

I think this was acted by _____

I think this was acted by _____

I think this was acted by _____

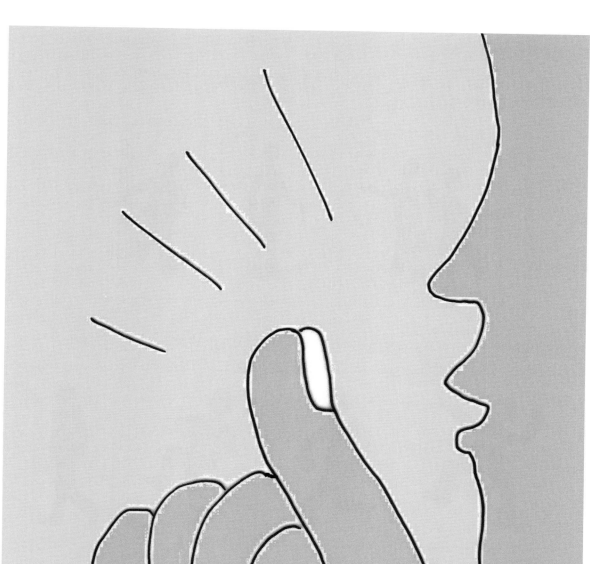

Act it out – Checklist

How do you enter the room? Together? One after each other? Does one of you get called into the room?

What would the person you are acting be feeling: excited/angry/happy/sad...

Would they be moving fast or slow?

Act it out – Checklist

Would they be carrying something?

Would they be seated or standing?

Would they be behaving very friendly and informal or polite and formal?

Act it out – Checklist

Would they be talking? How can we mime (i.e. say something without sound) talking?

What would they be doing with their hands?

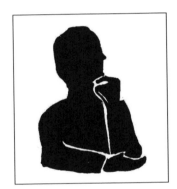 

Act it out – Everyday social problems

Somebody makes you a cake but you don't like people singing 'Happy Birthday' – it makes you feel too shy. How could you tell people this?

You are at the dentist and want him to stop because you need to cough. What can you do/ say?

You have bought a new kettle and it doesn't work. What would you say to the shop assistant when you take it back?

Act it out – Everyday social problems

You are given a birthday present that you already have. How could you communicate this while still remaining polite?

You are disappointed with your new hair cut. How can you complain to the hairdresser and what could you ask them to do to make it better?

You are in the middle of an interview and your mobile phone goes off. What can you say/do?

2.4 Board Game Builder

Competitive games that work with both luck and skill levels differentiated to the players are fair and motivating and encourage a greater awareness of sharing 'social space' and turn taking. A game made by the players means more, is more significant and more motivating than one from the box. It can be made to a much larger scale than a small boxed game, which makes it physically and visually more accessible – students will feel fully immersed in it. This activity works well for either a craft-based group to make from scratch or could be integrated as a team task within a communication group or as a stand-alone session to increase awareness of each other's skills and interests and encourage cooperation between learners.

The mechanics of the game itself are simple old-fashioned snakes and ladders; everyone knows the rules, and can be encouraged to count along the squares. By having a differentiated question on every square, players are pulled into participation at a level meaningful to them. At any one point the focus on the game is not just on the player moving the dice but also engages alternating 'quizmasters' to choose a question for the player and decide if the player is right. This higher level of participation again keeps people watching the player moving the dice to see which colour they will land on.

Aims

- Develop awareness of other members of the group.

- Practise number skills 1–6.

- Create an opportunity to cooperate with others to make and play a board game.

- Identify own and others' areas of knowledge and interest.

- Practise assembly and creativity techniques.

Resources

- 4 large sheets of card (A2 size, though they will be trimmed square) – this will make a good-size game to spread on a large table or have players seated around it with the game on the floor.

- Large dice.

- A selection of inflated and deflated balloon outlines printed on card (at least one for each learner).

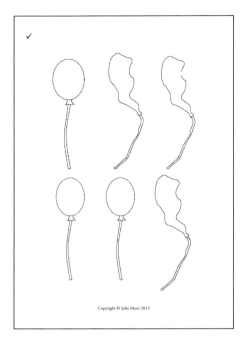

- A selection of pens/glitter/glue/paint/collage materials, depending on time and resources.

- Marker pen and ruler.

- One copy of the numbers 1–49 (for a reasonably fast-paced game).

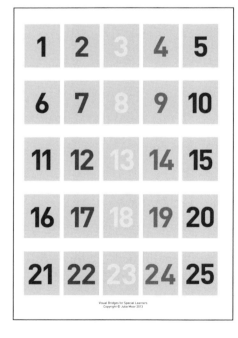

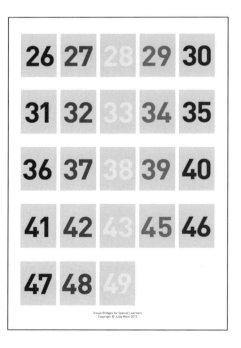

- Five copies of the coloured markers (i.e. five lots of each colour).

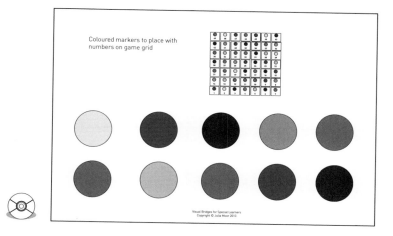

- One copy of 'The Rules'.

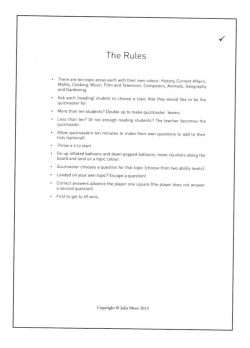

- One copy of the questions (ten categories).

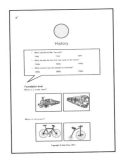  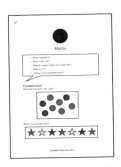 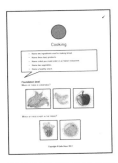 

  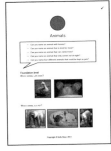 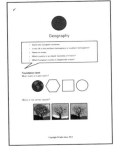 

Prior to the activity

- Trim and tape together the four large sheets of card and trim to make a large square.

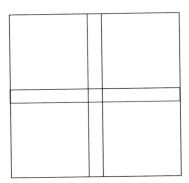

- On the front of the boards – mark out 7 × 7 squares.

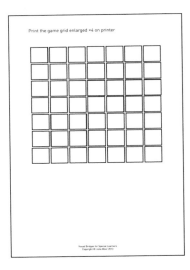

- You may choose to print the pre-printed grid out on four sheets of A4 – this would assemble large enough for up to five players.

- Print off a set of question sheets.

Delivering the activity

Talk to the group about their knowledge strengths; we all have some knowledge about the areas of life that interest us. Ask the group about their interests and discuss how we can use them to make a game that shares our knowledge within the group. We will be looking at the diverse areas of: History, Current Affairs, Maths, Cooking, Music, Film and Television, Computers, Animals, Geography and Gardening.

This is a good opportunity for students to share knowledge personal to them – often students can surprise with an in-depth interest in a very specific area.

Each knowledge category has a colour and students will then start to assemble the game by gluing a number and a colour to each individual square; colours can be random, numbers will go from 1–49 as follows:

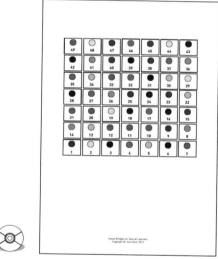

Allocate an amount of time for decorating the inflated and deflated balloons; you may wish to use one colour for inflated and another for deflated. Ask the group, to make them feel involved in the design and appearance of their game.

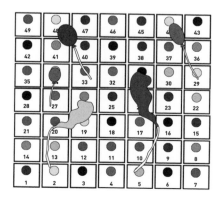

Ask students to arrange the cut-out balloons onto the game, making sure that the numbers on the squares are still visible. You may need to shorten balloon strings or extend them with a pen. Before these are stuck down check with the group if the way they are placed is fair. Confirm that counters landing on the end of an inflated balloon will go up the board and those on a deflated balloon will have to go down.

The Rules

Run through 'The Rules' with the group to ensure everyone knows what they are doing.

Ask reading students to choose a topic from the above by identifying areas they would like to quiz their fellow players on – they will then be the quizmaster for that topic area.

Whenever a player's counter lands on a colour, the quizmaster for that topic will ask the player a question (they may need support to choose an appropriate level for the player). For example, if the player chooses 'Cooking', the quizmaster could ask any one of the spoken questions in the call-out box or could choose a foundation-level question where the player is asked to identify the answer using the picture clues (they could point, speak or gesture). If they are correct then the player can move on one square.

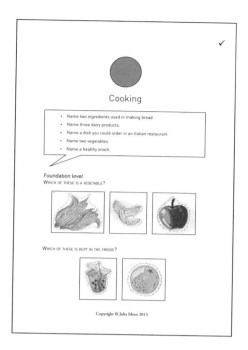

If some students wish to share asking questions from the same topic, that is fine. If students wish to make up their own questions related to the topic, then this is also fine. Correct answers advance the player one square (the player does not answer a second question). If a player lands on his or her own topic colour then the player misses answering the question.

The objective for the session leader is to try to pull the group into participating to a much greater extent than students would in a normal turn-taking game, this keeps students interested in both the topics and tracking how others are doing. Don't forget to use the game to practise numeracy (e.g. by asking students to identify what number they would like to throw, etc.).

Differentiation and development

- For every category there are two levels of question, the easiest being to identify a picture. The range of difficulty means that most players should feel engaged and capable of being successful.

- Because the board is made by students, the game could be made as big or as tactile as possible to assist those with visual impairments. Suggestions would be to use different materials for inflated and deflated balloons or use actual deflated balloons and ping-pong balls to represent inflated ones. Tactile materials can be used to represent different categories of questions and could be craft foam/felt/ribbed card/Wikki Stix (wax craft sticks that can be bent into any shape and secured to the board) or any number of household materials (bottle tops and caps, etc.). Question sheets should be printed in an accessible font size and Braille readers should have a question sheet in Braille.

- Once the board has been made, the question categories can change according to the areas being studied or the ability of the whole group, and can be used time and again to bring a topic into the spotlight using a familiar and comfortable format.

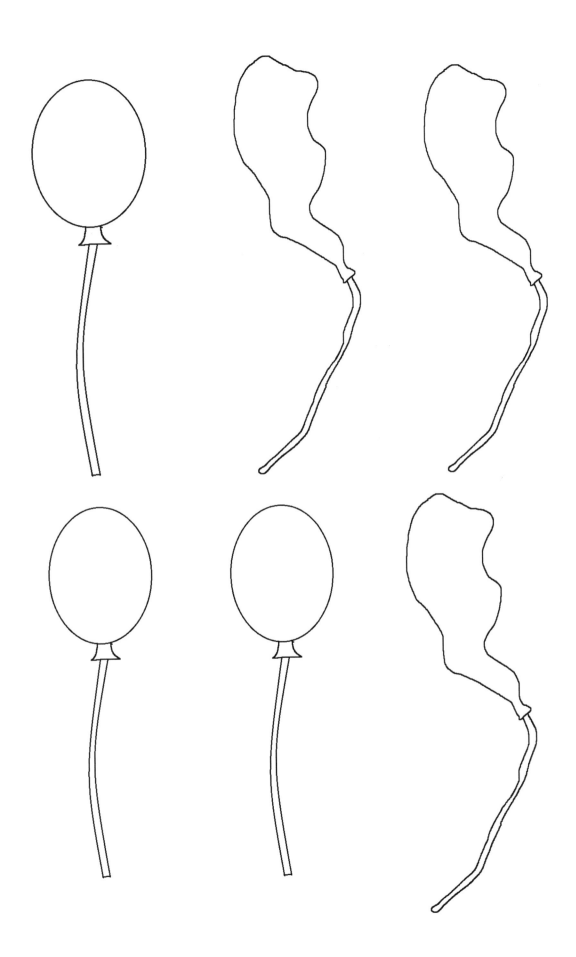

The Rules

- There are ten topic areas each with their own colour: History, Current Affairs, Maths, Cooking, Music, Film and Television, Computers, Animals, Geography and Gardening.

- Ask each (reading) student to choose a topic that they would like to be the quizmaster for.

- More than ten students? Double up to make quizmaster 'teams'.

- Less than ten? Or not enough reading students? The teacher becomes the quizmaster.

- Allow quizmasters ten minutes to make their own questions to add to their lists (optional).

- Throw a 6 to start.

- Go up inflated balloons and down popped balloons, move counters along the board and land on a topic colour.

- Quizmaster chooses a question for that topic (choose from two ability levels).

- Landed on your own topic? Escape a question!

- Correct answers advance the player one square (the player does not answer a second question).

- First to get to 49 wins.

History

- When did World War Two end?

  1900   1945   1899

- What decade did the first man land on the moon?

  1960s   1860s   1990s

- What century was the telephone invented?

  1600s   1800s   1900s

Foundation level

WHICH IS A STEAM TRAIN?

   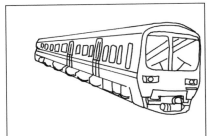

WHICH IS THE OLDEST?

Current Affairs

- Who is the current US president?
- Who is the current UK prime minister?
- Name a daily newspaper.
- Name a celebrity in the news at the moment.

Foundation level

WHICH ARE THE NEWSPAPERS?

WHICH IS THE NEWS PROGRAMME?

Maths

- What is double 15?
- What is 100 – 30?
- What do I need to add to 65 to make 100?
- What is 7 x 7?
- Can you count backwards from 5?

Foundation level

HOW MANY BLUE SPOTS ARE THERE?

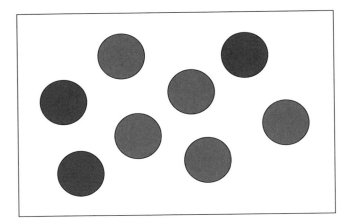

WHICH COLOUR COMES NEXT?

Cooking

- Name two ingredients used in making bread.
- Name three dairy products.
- Name a dish you could order in an Italian restaurant.
- Name two vegetables.
- Name a healthy snack.

Foundation level

WHICH OF THESE IS A VEGETABLE?

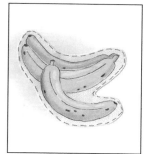

WHICH OF THESE IS KEPT IN THE FRIDGE?

Music

- Can you name a string instrument?

- Can you name an instrument you would play by blowing into it?

- Can you name a track by the band 'Abba'?

- What does 'CD' stand for?

- Can you finish this sentence: 'The Phantom of the...'

Foundation level

WHICH OF THESE INSTRUMENTS IS A GUITAR?

WHICH INSTRUMENT DO YOU SHAKE?

Film and Television

- Can you name a soap opera?
- Can you name a Disney film?
- Can you name a Harry Potter film?
- Can you name the TV presenter for your favourite programme?
- Can you name a TV talent programme?

Foundation level

WHICH IS A REMOTE CONTROL?

WHAT IS THE LISTENING EQUIPMENT CALLED THAT FITS TO YOUR HEAD?

✓

Computers

- Can you name a social network?
- Can you name a search engine?
- Can you name an internet shop?
- What does WWW stand for?
- Does email need a stamp?

Foundation level
WHERE IS THE KEYBOARD?

WHERE IS THE SCREEN?

Animals

- Can you name an animal with hooves?
- Can you name an animal that is bred for meat?
- Can you name an animal that can climb trees?
- Can you name an animal that only comes out at night?
- Can you name four different animals that could be kept as pets?

Foundation level

WHICH ANIMAL LAYS EGGS?

WHICH ANIMAL IS A PET?

Geography

- Name two European countries.
- Is the UK in the northern hemisphere or southern hemisphere?
- Name an ocean.
- Which country is an island: Australia or France?
- Which European country is shaped like a boot?

Foundation level

WHAT SHAPE IS PLANET EARTH?

WHICH IS THE HOTTEST SEASON?

Gardening

- In which season do trees lose their leaves?
- Can you name a yellow flower?
- Name two things that plants need.
- Why do plant pots need to have a hole in the base?
- Can you name a spring flower?

Foundation level

WHICH OF THESE FLOWERS IS A DAISY?

WHICH OF THESE CAN YOU NOT EAT?

 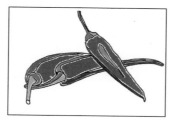 

2.5 A Flock of Poems

There are many barriers to creative writing for all kinds of students: not knowing where to start or how to structure a piece of creative writing, what to write about, or why to write in the first place. Yet once writers start to see successful results, work they are proud to share, then confidence rockets and motivation to keep writing is fuelled. Other students may have verbal ideas but have little opportunity to express these in written or visual form. Using the template will enable even the most reluctant writers to have a go. The students will be encouraged to think about and find words to describe the things in life that *they* enjoy, for example a warm flask of tea on a chilly beach, and use these same words to describe a person, place, object or animal in their life that makes them feel good. This positive content promotes students to focus on life-affirming language, thoughts and memories and to think about the little things in their daily lives as part of the bigger picture of 'good' things to celebrate.

This activity works well with a group of 'beginner writers', from students able to copy or trace letters to those able to generate and write their own words. The template enables all students a degree of success and takes writers through stages to generate an imaginative and successful poem. The presentation of the poems as a 'flock' encourages writers to look at others' work and to view their own contribution as an essential part of the whole project. The activity can also accommodate non-writers through using collage.

Aims

- Develop creative language.

- Develop imagination skills.

- Practise and develop literacy skills at several ability levels.

- Create the opportunity to cooperate with others on a task.

- Develop and promote reflection on positive feeling.

Resources

- The sample poem to read to the group.

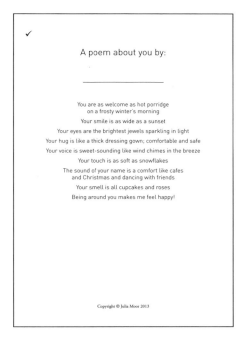

- A poem template (one copy for each student) – either A4 version or large text version (which is available on the CD).

- Bird mounts on A2 card (one for each student).

Copyright © Julia Moor 2013

Or, if resources do not allow, print the small birds on A4 for the students to cut out and lay over and around the edges of the poem.

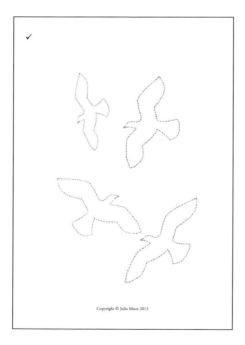

Copyright © Julia Moor 2013

- Pens, scissors and glue.

- Tactile objects to help discussion (optional) – a necklace/shell/piece of velvet/perfume/a flower/beads/a soft toy.

- A selection of magazines (to use as a collage expression for non-writers).

- A set of the 6 adjectives ideas cards printed from the CD.

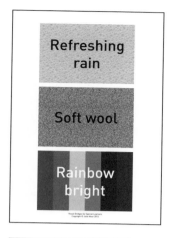

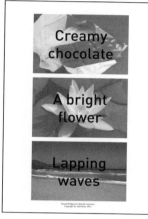

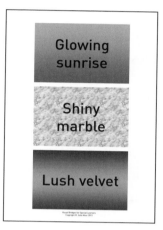

Prior to the activity

- Print out the bird outline enlarged onto four sheets. Most printers will enable you to enlarge the image to A2 poster size and print it over four A4 pages.

- Assemble the pieces and trace the bird outline onto A2 card. Alternatively draw the bird outline freehand directly onto the card and cut out the bird-shaped aperture using a knife and a cutting mat, or you could use scissors (start from the centre and work outwards). This will create a mount for the poem. You will need a mount for each student.

- Also print a poem template on paper – one for each student. There are two templates to choose from – one to describe a favourite person or animal and one to describe a favourite place.

- Print off the adjectives ideas cards and mount on card or laminate for durability.

Delivering the activity

Lead the group into discussion… What is poetry? Can we all be creative? Can we all write poetry? Does all poetry have to rhyme? Can writing make us feel good?

Read the sample poem (created using the template). Who could the poem be about? A best friend, a relative or parent? Someone the writer clearly likes. Let the group know that they can all write something similarly creative with a little imagination – it's just a case of getting started.

Explain to the group that they are going to make poetry using a template. The students will need to think about positive describing words (adjectives) such as soft/bright/pretty. They can have in mind a person, animal or place that makes them feel good.

Discuss adjectives – pass around a selection of real items (a necklace/shell/piece of velvet/perfume/a flower/beads/a soft toy) and ask the students to try to find words to describe them.

Now pass the adjectives ideas cards around – do they help to describe the items?

Place all the ideas cards in the centre of the table.

Hand out a copy of the poem template to each student and check that they all have a person, animal, or place to write about.

Students then fill in the template using the ideas cards. Depending on ability and literacy level students can either write or type the entire poem, complete the template either independently or copy their own dictated ideas, or complete the template using pictures torn from magazines.

Mount the bird aperture over the students' finished poems and secure with two-sided tape, or if working on a smaller scale, overlay cut-out birds onto the poem.

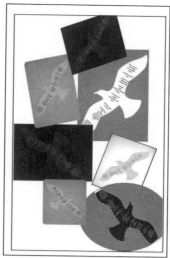

Allow plenty of time for students to look at each other's work and/or read out their poems. Explain that people come in all shapes and sizes, like birds, and that together they can work as a group, a flock, to showcase something pretty impressive. The collection of birds can then be either displayed as a flock or photographed.

Differentiation and development

- The adjectives ideas cards are to assist students who need some literacy support; if you feel your students would prefer to generate their own ideas then leave out the cards.

- Assess the literacy level of each student and decide how they would prefer to construct their poem:

  - Handwrite.

  - Type.

  - Dictate ideas and then copy them out.

  - Some students may wish to write single adjectives directly onto the cut-out bird.

- Some students may want to use pictures instead of words – present a selection of magazines and ask them to cut out and paste all the images they feel positive about. Mount the bird aperture over the top.

- Remember to use the large text version of the template for students who need a larger area to work with or who may have vision difficulties.

- This poem activity could be used to springboard a range of creative writing activities through exploring adjectives as follows:

  - Ask students to choose a 'scene' postcard and ask them to describe the scene using either the adjectives ideas cards or template if needed.

  - Allow students to develop their own templates/ideas and images. They may wish to use themed mounts (autumn/holidays/sea) and creative ideas.

A poem about you by:

_____

You are as welcome as hot porridge
on a frosty winter's morning

Your smile is as wide as a sunset

Your eyes are the brightest jewels sparkling in light

Your hug is like a thick dressing gown; comfortable and safe

Your voice is sweet-sounding like wind chimes in the breeze

Your touch is as soft as snowflakes

The sound of your name is a comfort like cafes
and Christmas and dancing with friends

Your smell is all cupcakes and roses

Being around you makes me feel happy!

A poem about you by:

_____

You are as welcome as

_____

Your smile is as

_____

Your eyes are

_____

Your hug is like

_____

Your voice is sweet-sounding like

_____

Your touch is as soft as

_____

The sound of your name is a comfort like

_____

Your smell is

_____

Being around you makes me feel

_____

Thank you

A poem about my favourite place:

_____

You are as welcoming as

_____

The first glimpse of you is as beautiful as

_____

The air around is as fresh as

_____

The sky above you is as clear as

_____

The ground around you is as safe as

_____

Your smell takes me back to

_____

Your memories to me are

_____

I hear around me

_____

The sound of your name is a comfort like

_____

Being here makes me feel

_____

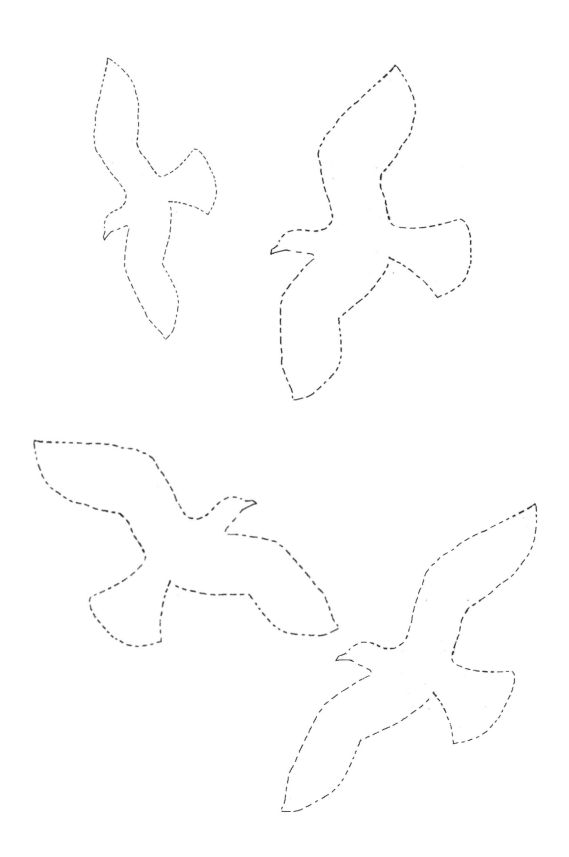

2.6 Meal Maker

This activity could be used as a learning and cooperation task to complement a healthy eating or meal planning group, or as a stand-alone activity to increase awareness of each other and practise working in teams.

Aims

- Develop an awareness of other members of the group.

- Practise fine motor skills, cutting and assembling.

- Create the opportunity to identify individual skills within a group.

- Create an opportunity to communicate around food.

- Opportunity to develop knowledge of healthy diets and food categories.

Resources

- There are 11 colour sheets of food images in large size on the CD or three sheets of smaller food images, which you can either photocopy in black and white from the book or print in colour from the CD. Students who struggle to decode language and pictures will be more successful and more motivated working with colour prints if time and resources allow.

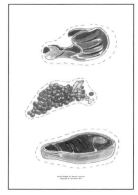

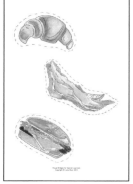

Meal maker food choices –
Select, cut and assemble

Copyright © Julia Moor 2013

Meal maker food choices –
Select, cut and assemble

Copyright © Julia Moor 2013

Meal maker food choices –
Select, cut and assemble

Copyright © Julia Moor 2013

- Glue sticks.

- Scissors.

- Prints of sample meals.

- A plate for each team.

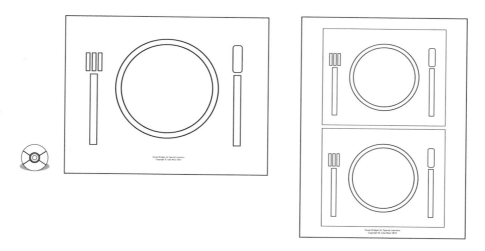

- Differentiated activities as listed below.

Prior to the activity

Gather together resources and print picture sheets and differentiated resources.

Delivering the activity

Commence a discussion about balanced eating, meal planning and so on. Identify if anyone struggles to eat enough fruit and vegetables. Offer suggestions for how this can be addressed (juices/soups/smoothies). Who is involved in planning their own meals? What difficulties arise in doing this – budgets, lack of ideas, cooking challenges? Discuss the problems that may arise when a meal is served for a group of people with different tastes and how compromises can be made (e.g. serving sauces on the side). Talk about food likes and dislikes, look at common likes and dislikes and more unusual tastes. Don't forget to use the picture resources to supplement the conversation.

Explain how the following activity will look at planning a menu for a group of people – we need to be aware not just what is healthy but what other people's tastes are. Ask students to pretend that they are living in groups of two or three (depending on the size of the group) and will need to plan a day's food together.

What questions should we ask each other? Ask for suggestions from the group and then put forward the following:

- Are you allergic to any foods?

- Are there any foods you dislike?

- Are you on a special diet or trying to lose weight?

Each small group will need to establish between them a breakfast, a lunch and an evening meal that they would all enjoy and that they feel between them would be healthy – remind the group that some treats are fine but the key is balance, so if they decide on a blow-out breakfast then they may want to choose a light lunch or if they have a dessert at lunch then they may want to consider fruit for dessert at evening meal. They will then present this on a series of plates to the rest of the group who will mark the menu out of ten.

Provide each small group with a set of printed plates and foods (large or small scale depending on students' fine motor skills/vision), scissors and glue sticks. Allow the group a set time period (around 15 minutes) to talk to each other and select a breakfast with the the appropriate photos. Ask them to identify who will cut the items out, who will stick them down and who will present the meal to the group at the end. Remind students to tidy away scrap paper as they go along (you may want to set aside unused food pictures to use as a development idea later). Repeat the process for lunch and evening dinner.

Regroup everyone and ask each small group to take turns to present their menu, ask students to look for balance between the three meals, how appealing the plates look, sensible amounts of food and count the portions of fruit and vegetables over the day. For extra fun and a competitive edge, ask the group to score each menu out of ten on score cards.

Differentiation and development

- The activity can be printed on a large scale or smaller scale (the black and white photocopiable version is small scale). Choose large scale printing on heavyweight card for students whose physical difficulties may be problematic.

- For students who may struggle to offer their own suggestions, provide a suggested meal idea. These students can then use this as a select, match and assemble activity.

- Braille users could assemble a plate with food labels in Braille.

- For students working on literacy, offer some written meal ideas for them to select matching picture foods. Or ask students to write food names on the blank plates.

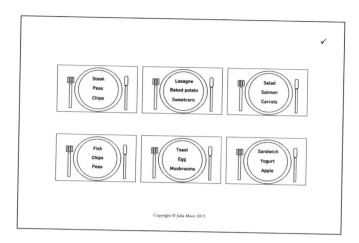

- Some students may enjoy the challenge of being asked to create a day's menu for a vegetarian or someone unable to eat dairy. For numeracy work, learners may wish to create a menu for someone on a diet of 1500 calories a day – provide calculators, scrap paper and a calorie conversion book.

- You may wish to photograph the finished meal plates for students with severe communication difficulties to use for choice making as part of a picture exchange programme.

- As a development and extension task the spare food pictures can be categorised into dairy, carbohydrates, fruit, vegetables and protein. Students working at a more advanced level can then extend and develop their knowledge of healthy eating and food categories.

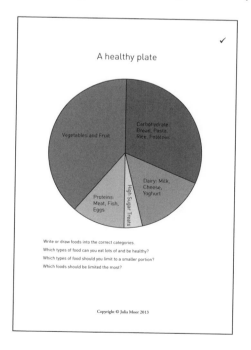

Meal maker food choices –
Select, cut and assemble

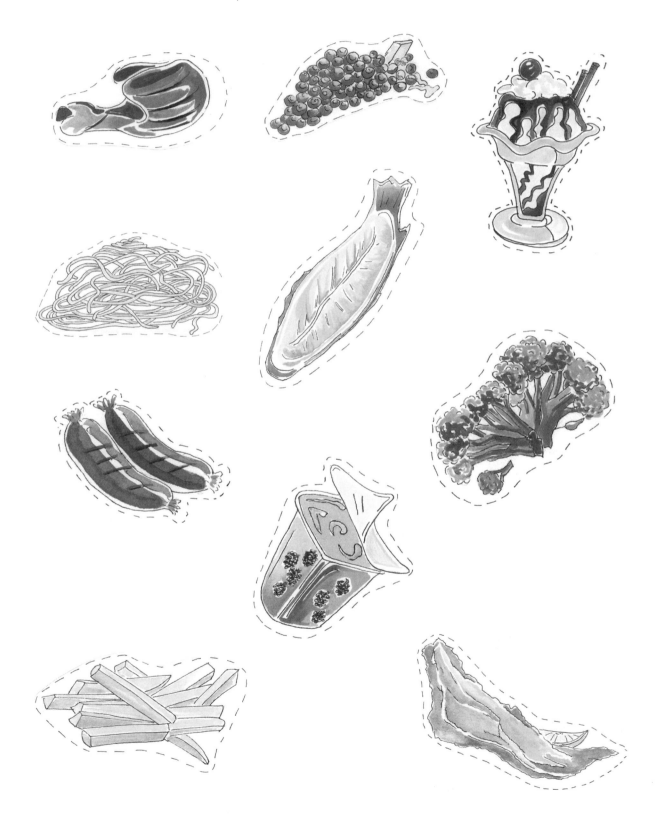

Meal maker food choices –
Select, cut and assemble

Meal maker food choices –
Select, cut and assemble

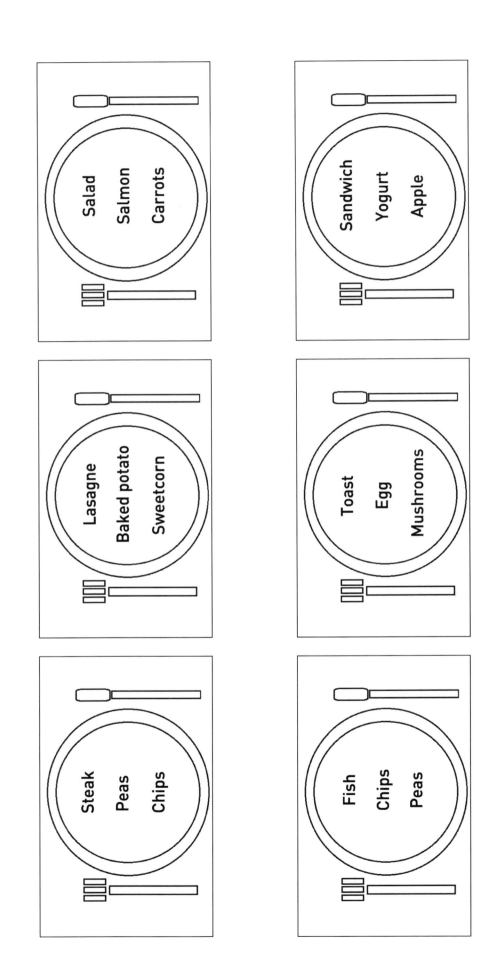

Salad
Salmon
Carrots

Sandwich
Yogurt
Apple

Lasagne
Baked potato
Sweetcorn

Toast
Egg
Mushrooms

Steak
Peas
Chips

Fish
Chips
Peas

A healthy plate

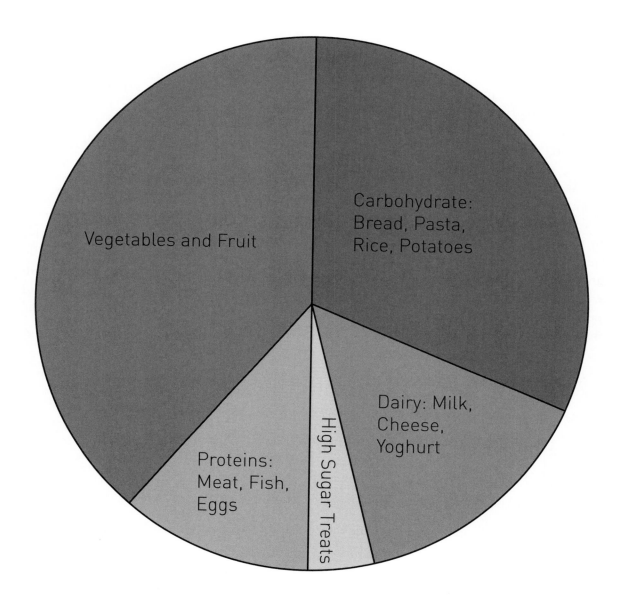

Vegetables and Fruit

Carbohydrate:
Bread, Pasta,
Rice, Potatoes

Dairy: Milk,
Cheese,
Yoghurt

Proteins:
Meat, Fish,
Eggs

High Sugar Treats

Write or draw foods into the correct categories.

Which types of food can you eat lots of and be healthy?

Which types of food should you limit to a smaller portion?

Which foods should be limited the most?

2.7 Collage Race

This activity gets people 'doing' and talking; it's a good initial assessment activity for session leaders to observe receptive language skills, interaction skills and practical skills. I find students enjoy the competitive nature of the 'race'. There is also an element of 'luck' in finding an appropriate item which builds in fairness and doesn't just put those students able to work quickly at an advantage.

At a creative level, collage making draws on visual inspiration, curiosity and reflective skills: reshaping images that already exist into a new form. Encouraging creative thought is a lifelong developing process for all of us but especially for learners where problem solving is a barrier in life. All decisions and actions in life are made easier and more enjoyable with a creative mindset. The task element of the 'Collage Race' is a means to get learners started on selecting and assembling images. All being well, your group will then want to take this further with more of their own creative input and a piece of work that reflects the visual material they find personally appealing and meaningful. Remember to squirrel away lots of printed visual material in the weeks preceding the activity so that your group has a large selection to choose from.

Aims

- Create an opportunity to work as a team.

- Develop observation and identification skills.

- Practise following instructions.

- Create the opportunity to identify practical strengths.

- Create an opportunity for artistic interpretation and creativity.

Resources

- A collection of magazines and images – try to find a mix of general interest and specialist hobby ones (e.g. cars/gardening/cooking). Put out a request a week or so before the activity and check out local libraries which often have a magazine recycle box. You could also bring in catalogues, leaflets, old books and a selection of images printed off the internet. Ensure that there is at least one picture element to match the items on the sheets.

- Scissors.

- Glue sticks.

- Printouts of the team sheets/collage grids (you could try printing these on 4 sheets of A4 to create a bigger area for a group to work around).

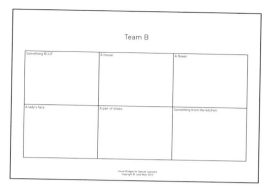

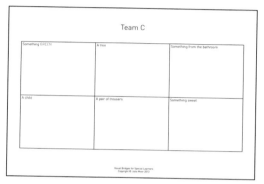

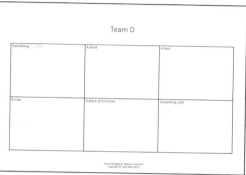

- A timer – either a kitchen timer, timer on a mobile phone or, if you have access to a computer/projector in the classroom, there are many online visual timers which would enable the whole group to see how much time they have.

Prior to the activity

Gather resources and produce collage grids by dividing a large sheet of paper (A2 or A3 or lining paper) into six squares and attaching one of the pre-printed grid headings in each square. Or you may choose to use the A4 picture version for students needing visual clues.

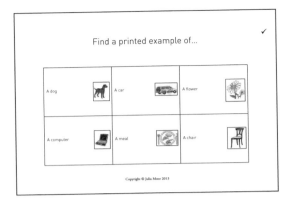
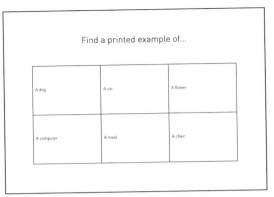

Delivering the activity

Talk to the group about competing in teams and start a discussion about team competitions such as sports activities. Ask the group if everyone working in a team does the same task or different ones; look at something like football as an example, for example a goalkeeper, a striker, a defender.

Discuss general skills around the table (e.g. cooking/art) followed by looking at skills specific to the game Collage Race, who is good at listening, reading, cutting and assembling, directing tasks, following instructions?

Define the term 'collage' to learners as a collection of images put together on one page to make a picture and show the group the sample collage (or make your own). Ask students to identify the elements in the picture; you can also talk about where things are found, what colour they are and their function. Remember to make the prior discussion motivating and engaging to pull learners in ready to participate. When learners begin to see the activity as meaningful and relevant they will be more ready to engage than if they are just handed an activity and a set of instructions.

The group will then need to be divided into teams. This will depend on the number and nature of the learners, and you may want to just split into pairs for a small group or maybe have four teams of four for a larger one. You could allocate teams or select randomly. Hand each team a 'collage grid' and give them five minutes to decide:

- Who will read out the separate elements on the collage grid to the group?

- Who will look through and research the magazines for items to match?

- Who will cut the images from the magazines?

- Who will glue in the appropriate grid?

The group will be racing against the clock so make sure everyone has decided who is doing which task and has the right equipment to do this before setting the timer (suggestion: 30–45 minutes depending on learners). The pile of image resources should be accessible to all the groups at once.

Your timer could be anything from an online visual timer projected onto the wall to a kitchen timer.

As the activity gets under way remind learners to return magazines to the centre when they have used them. When the first team completes their collage, stop the clock and note their time (to a round of applause), then restart and allow all the teams to complete. At the end of the activity, review all the collages and check that each element is present and correct. Ask students to identify what they enjoyed/disliked about the activity and which tasks they found difficult or easy. This will help you plan this activity a second time around and give learners the opportunity to feed back their comments.

Differentiation and development

- At a foundation level, if students need picture cues, use the differentiated sheet and only expect one example of each image per square (you may also choose to remove two squares to reduce the task to four images).

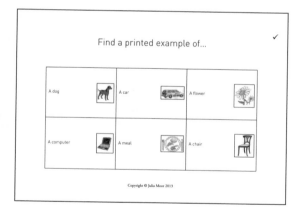

- For students working at a higher level of motor skills ability, set the task with a creative element and ask the team to think about how they will assemble their work. They may use multiple images, overlap elements and generally work at not only identifying and using specified images but on creating an appealing piece of artwork with them. Supply frame mounts to complete the work and again experiment on where to place the mount for the best effect. Collages can have a dream-like feel where images flow from one to the other. This can be achieved by choosing larger images to form the background and overlapping joins with smaller more intricately cut-out images which pull the picture together and link the elements.

- Finished collages could be taken further by scanning and manipulating images on the computer – students could use a free online picture editing tool to produce creative colour effects. You could also make prints of each of the teams' work and ask them to identify the elements in each other's collages.

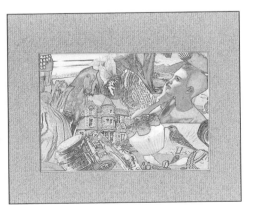

- The collage work can be developed as extensively as the artistic and creativity skills of the individual students wish to take it. Highly motivated individuals may wish to trace over their assembled collage and paint an original piece of modern art. Learners with specialist interests may wish only to focus on images of one type, for example trains or movies – give your learners time and opportunity to take this as far as they are able.

Find a printed example of...

A flower	A car	A dog
A chair	A meal	A computer

2.8 Team Art

Sometimes my students join creativity sessions with trepidation; they may have initially liked the sound of signing up but then concern themselves that they may not be 'good enough' or don't think they have any 'arty' ideas. This team activity brings everyone together on an artistic level and showcases how presenting different media side by side can have great results. It allows students to experiment with materials without the pressure of having to make something individually and gets students communicating around colour and pattern. It also gives the teacher/session leader the opportunity to identify what level and type of support is required by individuals and which media and style of working they prefer.

Aims

- Develop fine motor and mark making skills.

- Create an opportunity to interact with different creative media.

- Create an opportunity to use colour and pattern imaginatively.

- Develop awareness of, and communication with, other members of the group.

Resources

- Prints of the various turtle shapes as follows (these can be found on the CD).

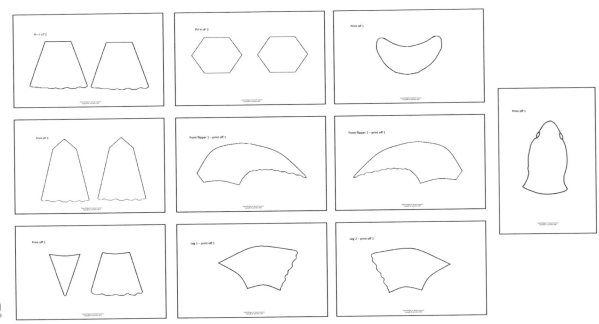

- A range of art media and equipment; this will be dictated by resources/time, the environment and student ability level. Read through the activity and suggestions before choosing your media.

- Large card (the turtle fits on 4 pieces of A2 card); you may choose to recycle some board or use thick wallpaper lining to mount the various pieces on.

- Glue stick and scissors.

- Digital camera.

- Sample printed turtle.

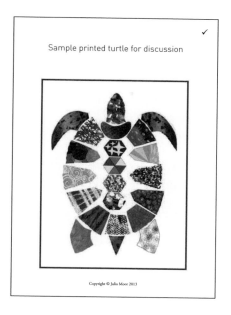

Sample printed turtle for discussion

Copyright © Julia Moor 2013

Prior to the activity

- Check you have all the section printouts – when arranged they should complete a turtle as shown.

- Gather and assemble various creative media (being mindful of time allowed and student abilities).

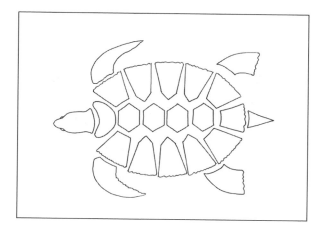

Delivering the activity

Ask students if they ever panic at the thought of filling a blank page with something 'creative' or get lost for ideas. Remind them that this is common for everyone, no matter how good we are at art or how much we enjoy it. Explain that the session will be all about the process of making art, of using colour and pattern, but that the end result will come about due to our efforts as a group and that everyone needs to join in to make this happen. Show students the sample turtle artwork photograph and allow them to evaluate the work themselves. Which colours and patterns do they like? Can they identify shapes and patterns within the work? Can they guess at any media that may have been used?

Encourage students to engage with the turtle concept by explaining a little about the creature and its symbolism… The turtle moves at his own pace, he's sociable and likes to live in big groups and he has a superb method of protection without attacking. Everyone in the group will also be working at their own pace to make a piece of group work. Students can work on one, two or three segments of the turtle's shell (depending on the size of the group) using a variety of media and styles (as chosen by the session leader). Judge your learners: some may be overwhelmed by too much choice or distracted by the media themselves, some may wish to experiment with lots of different styles.

Suggestions include:

- Completing a section using doodle art (there are some colouring sections already created) – choose a level of detail suited to the student's fine motor skills.

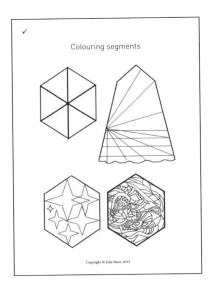

- Use cotton buds dipped in paint to make a dotted section.

- Use printing blocks and paint.

- Create wax resist patterns using crayons and water based paints (rubbing plates works well for the wax).

- Set up photography of shells/leaves/flowers, for example, and cut to the segment shapes.

- Overlap coloured tissues to create subtle shade effects.

- Marbled sheets of A4 and use the segments as a pattern to cut to size. (Marbling is achieved by floating oil-based paints onto a tray of water and dipping the sheets on top.

Demonstrate this activity first to your students and experiment using bought marbling paints or ordinary oil paints thinned with spirit.)

- Use felts/pencils/black liners for free-form patterns.

- Use the 'paint' package on a computer to create pattern sheets that can be cut to size using the segment shapes as templates.

- Use finger paints/splatter paints.

- Collage the segments using magazine images/internet images of specialist interests or even photos of each other.

- Place the segment in a tray/bottom of a large tin and drop marbles covered in paint and roll over the paper to create patterns.

- Use spirographs/stencils.

The suggestions are endless!

When all the segments are finished they can be assembled and pasted to card to make the complete turtle. Write a letter as follows on the back of each section to make assembly easier.

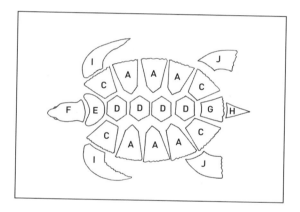

Differentiation and development

- Enable success by carefully tailoring the art technique and medium to your student's ability. Remember to secure work to the table for students with motor difficulties and allow individuals to have plenty of work space.

- The whole project could be made as a tactile artwork for visually impaired students by changing the media – some suggestions are:

  ◦ string dropped onto adhesive

  ◦ beads and buttons

  ◦ embossed segments

  ◦ fabrics, felts and textured papers

  ◦ threaded beads arranged to outline the segment

  ◦ craft sands and glitters

- ○ 3D textile paint used to fill segments with dots

- ○ scrunched tissues and foils

- ○ air-drying clay or papier mâché textured using clay tools

- ○ small shells/glass stones

- ○ mouldable wax craft sticks.

- Segments would need to be made out of heavyweight card or thin ply so students can examine and feel their shape. Temporarily arrange these into the turtle shape at the start of the project to support visually impaired students to understand what role their own piece will play in the final artwork. The finished piece will be substantial and should be displayed at a height where students can touch and interact with it.

- To enable everyone to take home a piece of the artwork you may choose to photograph the complete turtle and give everyone a print. There is lots of scope for development using the prints; students may go on to sketch/paint their own turtle images to mount alongside this. They may choose to pick one art style and create their own smaller version or mount multiple prints as a secondary piece of artwork.

- Students with access to IT may choose to try manipulating the photograph using a variety of photographic effects.

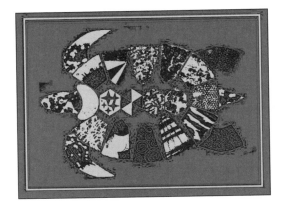

- For students on a creativity course sampling a full range of media, the turtle segment format could be used with clay segments or mounted textiles to make a group or individual piece of work. Often accredited art courses ask students to demonstrate a range of techniques and colour usage in a given media area; this is a great project to enable students to showcase their experiments.

Sample printed turtle for discussion

Colouring segments

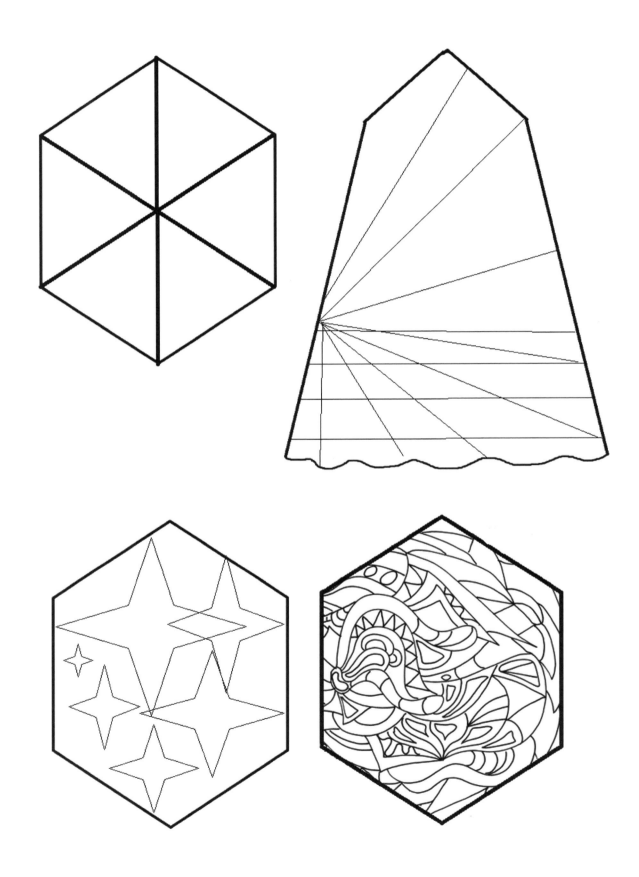

SECTION 3

Self-Awareness and Awareness of Others

Introduction

Activity 3.1 Awareness of Self and Others: First Impressions

Activity 3.2 Self-Awareness: My Choices – A Picture Preference Portrait

Activity 3.3 Self-Awareness: What am I Feeling? Identifying and Labelling Internal States

Activity 3.4 Self-Awareness: Understanding Me – Outside In

Activity 3.5 Self-Awareness: A Visual Strategy for Personal Goal-Setting

Activity 3.6 Awareness of Others: Using Preference Portraits to get to Know Others

Activity 3.7 Awareness of Others: Situations, Feelings, Actions

Activity 3.8 Awareness of Others: Different Perspectives

 All photocopiable sheets that accompany these activities can also be printed in colour from the CD at the back of the book. This icon denotes any sheets that can be found on the CD, but are not included in the book.

Introduction

Sadly, much of my students' personal time is taken up with the business of managing the functional impact of their disability on a day-to-day basis, leaving less capacity to invest in understanding both themselves and others. Disability struggles, practical issues, mental health problems and communication difficulties conspire to make understanding and expressing themselves and understanding their relationship dynamics problematic. My more passive students are willing to take a back seat when it comes to expressing choice and thinking about what makes them happy, allowing and sometimes preferring others to make guesses.

Understanding feelings, choices, goals and people requires a great deal of receptive and expressive language, which is why working on activities with a strong visual content is assistive in bridging the gap for those students struggling to process and decode language as well as express themselves. Visual prompts motivate and help struggling communicators to express an idea successfully. Once we create time and opportunity to do this and supplement communication barriers with visual cues, then individuals can get quite absorbed in rediscovering their preferences, choices and goals, comparing themselves to each other and analysing relationships.

This chapter assists students to look first at their own external and internal features before working at transferring this analysis to others around them. There are tools to assist students to express their preferences in the form of a Picture Preference Portrait and to use this tool to understand others. There are also visual strategies for goal setting. The chapter starts off with a gentle 'outside-in' approach to enthuse and encourage students to find the words to express more sensitive internal states, such as identifying individual strengths, and areas where support is needed for personal development.

3.1 Awareness of Self and Others
First Impressions

Like any set of learners, I find my students come in mixes of those who are very self-conscious and prefer not to have the spotlight over them and those who make full use of an opportunity to express an opinion or share an idea. This activity is a great way to encourage those more gregarious students to support the less bold to experiment with appearance, communicate with the rest of the group and participate at their most comfortable level, whether that be as a photographer, a dresser or a model. The activity enables students to have the opportunity to express themselves through outward appearance and to experiment with how they present to the rest of the world. This is a good warm-up activity to the section on self-awareness, to introduce students to reflecting on physical self, before moving on to awareness of internal states later in this section.

Aims

- Create an opportunity to experiment with appearance.

- Practise face-recognition skills.

- Sharpen awareness and observation of others.

- Create an opportunity to take photographs and reflect on own image.

Resources

- Prints of 'matching faces', one copy per student.

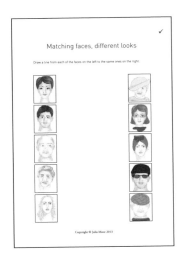

- Props – formal and casual hats/scarves/spectacles/sunglasses/costume jewellery.

- Face paints (optional).

- Handheld mirrors.

- Camera/tripod.

Prior to the activity

- Collect together the resources and equipment needed.

- Print off the 'matching faces' activity.

- Check you will have facilities to either print or view digital photos (if not, then this is a two-session project).

Delivering the activity

Start with a discussion about outward appearance... What physical aspects do we notice in others? For example, how many people in the group are wearing glasses? Who is wearing blue? Ask students if they have difficultly identifying faces if people change the way they look – perhaps put on a hat or change hairstyles. Often my students who are on the autistic spectrum find changes in the way people look particularly troublesome as attending to facial features can be uncomfortable. This is a quick and relatively easy start to the session and will help you assess individual difficulties in this area. The activity will also generate communication around appearance... Who prefers people not to wear sunglasses/hats that cover faces? Who likes experimenting with their appearance this way?

Complete the 'matching faces' activity first, giving learners time to work independently to match the faces that are the same. Regroup to discuss how each person has changed, for example added glasses, different hairstyle. Does this change who they are inside? Do the faces look more sophisticated/formal/relaxed, depending on how they are dressed? What are the learners' first impressions of each face and how does this change when the appearance changes? Do any of the faces look more approachable than others?

Introduce the props and ask students to select three items for *you*, the session leader, to wear. Solicit opinion about how this looks and support a learner to take a head/shoulders photograph of you. By this time, students have usually started to look through and handle the props. Give them plenty of time to get used to 'trying' and experimenting before asking for volunteers to allow themselves to be photographed.

The session can get as imaginative as students like; they may want to just try one adjustment (perhaps wear sunglasses) or go the full journey and wear painted clown make-up or a wig and party hat. The success of the activity is dependent not just on your learners' motivation to participate but on the range of resources you can find – hunt through charity shops/jumble sales and party shops. This is a resource that can be used for a variety of other communication/drama sessions.

Once you have a range of photos of your students in various guises, print them onto card (or paste onto card) and use in a variety of ways.

- **Pass round and identify**: Students select a card one at a time and hand it to the person they think is in the disguise.

- **Turn-taking card game**: Present the cards face down in a stack in the middle of the table and students take turns to turn over a card – if it is themselves, they can keep the card, if not, return it to the bottom of the stack and miss a turn. The first to uncover all pictures of themselves wins. (There will need to be at least four pictures of every student; you will also need to shuffle the main deck after every round.)

- **Matching**: At the simplest level the activity can be used as a match same to same picture activity or match black and white to colour.

Differentiation and development

This is a multi-sensory activity to encourage students to handle and experiment with the props and encourage visually impaired learners to share their ideas about how things feel.

- For learners struggling to match faces to their disguised pair on the 'matching faces' activity, print two sheets onto card and use as a straight matching same to same activity first.

- The session can be used as springboard to discussions and activities around creating a good first impression – take a range of formal and informal pictures and ask students to identify a look for an interview, a wedding and a fancy dress party.

- Students could try to alter *nothing but their expression* on each photo and then try to match feelings to photos. (You could link this to Activity 3.3.)

- Students might want to use their photos to produce a creative piece of work. These can be handled and discussed by all students who can give their feedback about a preferred 'look', or used to identify feelings.

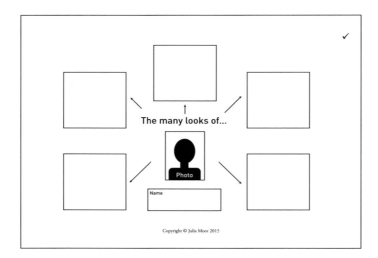

The many looks of…

Photo

Name

Matching faces, different looks

Draw a line from each of the faces on the left to the same ones on the right.

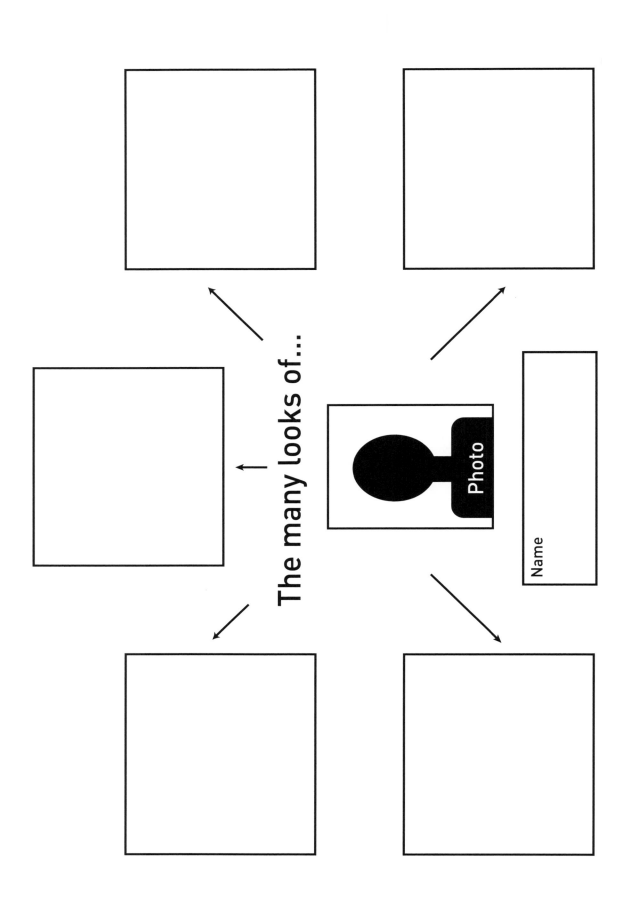

The many looks of....

Name

Photo

3.2 Self-Awareness
My Choices – A Picture Preference Portrait

Having a one-page portrait of your students' preferences will enable you to differentiate visual resources, discussion and activities to their own preferences and interests. It will allow you to know instantly if a student has a particular dislike to something and will give you key information that the student wishes you to know about him or herself.

The portrait can be as complex or as simple as the student feels comfortable with and will enable them to think about and express their preferences using lots of visual material about how they like to spend their time. Having an opportunity to express preference out of context supports students to feel their choices matter, increasing self-esteem and a sense of being valued.

I find students enjoy the hands on nature of selecting, cutting and sticking their preferences and dislikes; this style of activity encourages participation and motivates students to think about the visual content and what it represents.

Students can keep a copy of their portrait to take to different settings as a portable and accessible communication tool/interaction starting point. The portraits can also assist students to get to know each other (see Activity 3.6).

Aims

- Create the opportunity to express own preferences and dislikes about how to spend leisure time.

- Create the opportunity to reflect on and express preferred communication.

- Develop awareness of support needs.

- Practise fine motor skills in cutting and assembling.

Resources

- A blank copy of the preference portrait for each student.

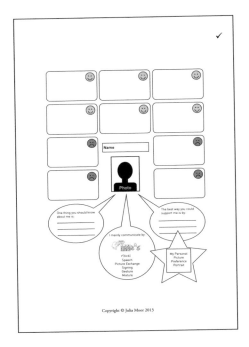

- A copy of the picture choices (3 x A4 sheets) for each student.

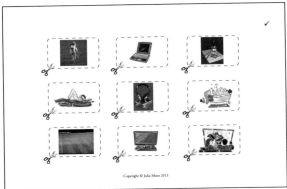

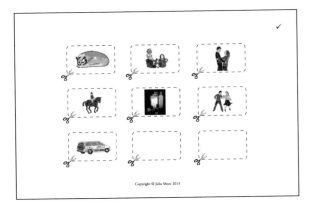

- A copy of Lucy's Picture Preference Portrait and 'What do we know about Lucy?' for each student.

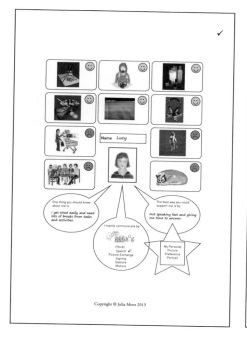
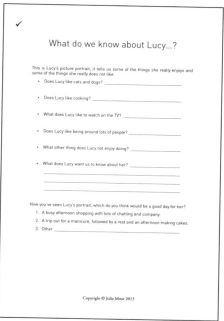

- Scissors, glue sticks, pens.

- Portrait photograph of each student (following consent).

Prior to the activity

- Print off the resources.

- Take and print off photographs of each student.

Delivering the activity

Hand the learners a copy of the complete portrait of 'Lucy' and ask them to take a few minutes to look and digest. Explain to students that this one sheet of paper tells us quite a lot about Lucy, the things she enjoys doing and the things that she doesn't like. It might not tell us everything but it's a start to getting to know her. Check students understand that the smiley and sad face emoticons represent like and dislike, and go through each photo checking students know what sort of activity it represents.

What is the most important thing that Lucy wants us to know about her? Remember this is not the same as being 'the most important thing about Lucy' – it's the one thing *she* would like people to know about her. Hand out the sheets 'What do we know about Lucy?' They can be completed individually and written or completed as a group during discussion.

Ask students if they feel it would be useful to have their own pen portrait, and to think about the sort of information they might like to include. Who do they think would benefit from seeing this and how might they benefit from having one? Do students think it would be a useful tool to get to know other people?

Allow plenty of time for learners to assemble their own visual or written pen portrait, adding internet images themselves if they need something specific.

When everyone has completed a pen portrait you may choose to use Activity 3.6 to show learners how to look at and understand each other's portrait.

Differentiation and development

- For students working on literacy, print off the pictures with written labels instead. Learners can then make the link between the picture and the written label and either copy the words only, or paste the picture and copy the word.

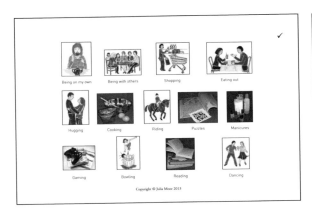 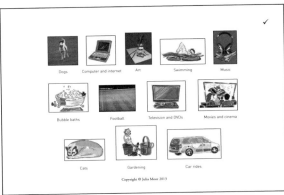

- Be mindful of learners with difficulties in assembling their portrait. Support could be in the form of holding paper to cut, or pre-cutting images, securing paper to the desk with masking tape, or enabling students to select through pointing.

- Students may need support to complete the three written sections by dictating or copying their own dictated ideas.

- IT students could use search engines to find logos, photos and images for choices that they have no illustration for.

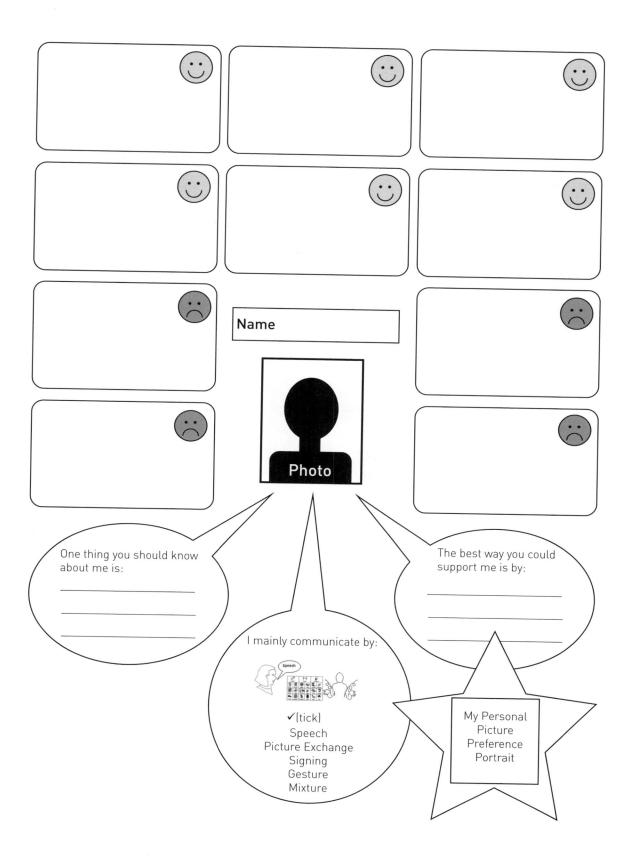

Name

Photo

One thing you should know about me is:

_____

_____

_____

The best way you could support me is by:

_____

_____

_____

I mainly communicate by:

✓(tick)
Speech
Picture Exchange
Signing
Gesture
Mixture

My Personal
Picture
Preference
Portrait

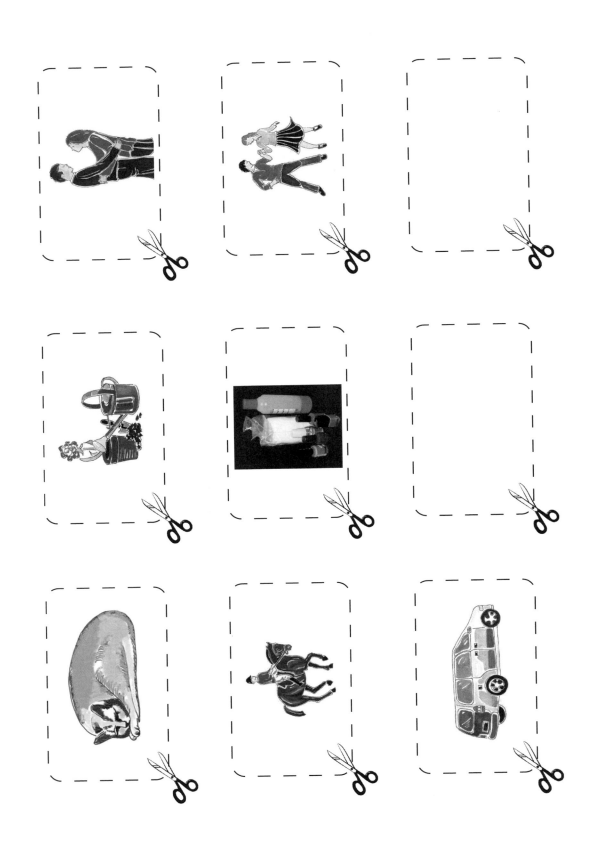

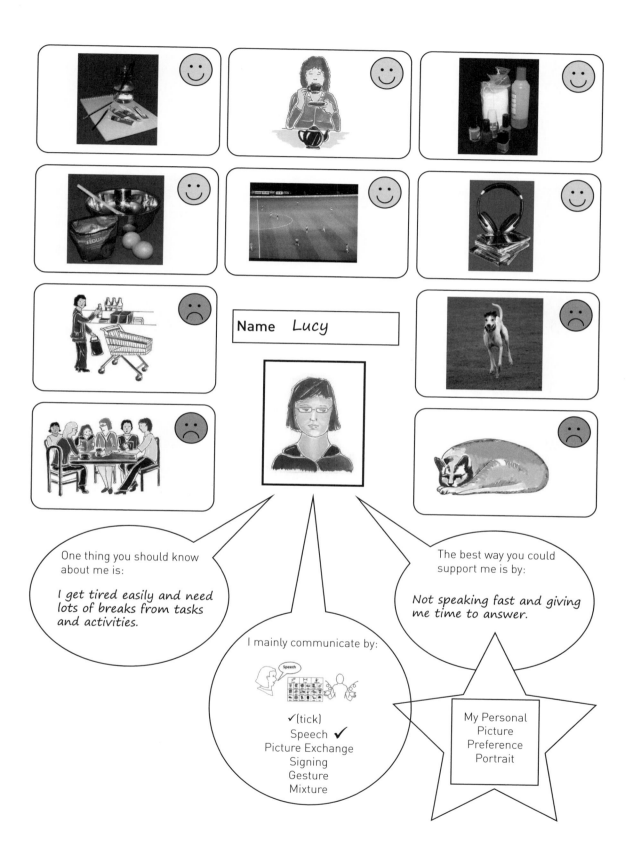

Name Lucy

One thing you should know about me is:

I get tired easily and need lots of breaks from tasks and activities.

The best way you could support me is by:

Not speaking fast and giving me time to answer.

I mainly communicate by:

✓(tick)
Speech ✓
Picture Exchange
Signing
Gesture
Mixture

My Personal Picture Preference Portrait

What do we know about Lucy...?

This is Lucy's picture portrait; it tells us some of the things she really enjoys and some of the things she really does not like.

- Does Lucy like cats and dogs? _____

- Does Lucy like cooking? _____

- What does Lucy like to watch on the TV? _____

- Does Lucy like being around lots of people? _____

- What other thing does Lucy not enjoy doing? _____

- What does Lucy want us to know about her? _____

  _____

  _____

  _____

Now you've seen Lucy's portrait, which do you think would be a good day for her?

1. A busy afternoon shopping with lots of chatting and company.

2. A trip out for a manicure, followed by a rest and an afternoon making cakes.

3. Other _____

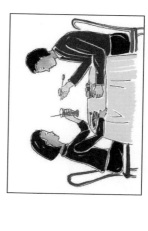

Eating out

Manicures

Dancing

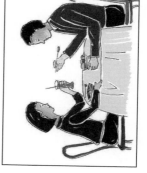

Shopping

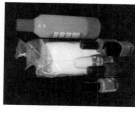

Puzzles

Reading

Riding

Being with others

Cooking

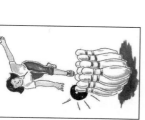

Bowling

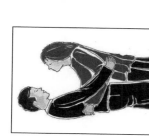

Being on my own

Hugging

Gaming

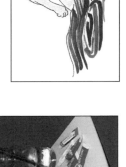

Music

Swimming

Art

Computer and internet

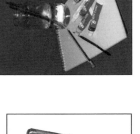

Dogs

Movies and cinema

Television and DVDs

Football

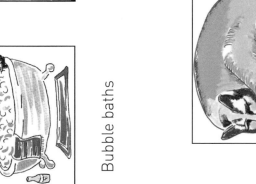

Bubble baths

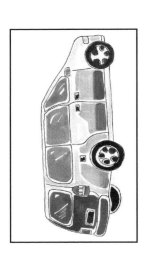

Car rides

Gardening

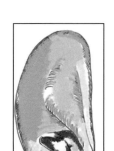

Cats

3.3 Self-Awareness
What am I Feeling? Identifying and Labelling Internal States

This is a foundation level emotion recognition activity to assist students to label and recognise their feelings – discuss how feelings physically feel, the sorts of situations where familiar feelings may arise and develop awareness of how to identify the feelings of others from clues in their facial expressions and behaviour. Many of my learners are able to reel off the labels for feelings but then struggle to identify a context when these feelings might exist or more importantly to recognise them in themselves as they unfold. The visual strategies help link a word label with how it feels, and act as a cognitive bridge.

Aims

- Develop awareness of the link between physical sensation and emotional state.

- Develop awareness of emotional reactions.

- Practise a strategy to control emotional reactions.

- Create awareness of when emotional support is needed.

Resources

- Copy of the picture feelings sheet (one per student).

- Copy of 2 scenarios sheets (one per student).

- Copy of feelings prompt sheet (as needed for reading students).

- Copy of 'Choose a feeling' sheet (one per student).

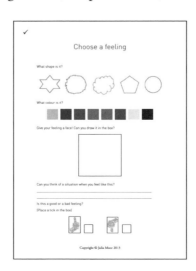

- Copy of the body printout (one per student).

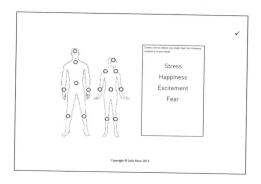

- Differentiated resources as described under Differentiation and development.

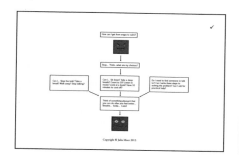
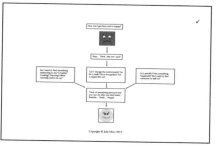

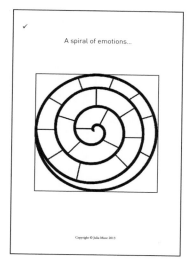

- Glue sticks/pens/pencils.

Prior to the activity

Print off resources as required including those for Differentiation and development as described below. If you are making matching or snap cards these need to be printed onto card.

Delivering the activity

Start with the picture feelings sheets to get conversation/words/gestures flowing...

As you pass these round (or project onto the wall if possible), learners will often start to verbalise their thoughts about each face and what it may be feeling. This will get students talking about feelings neutrally without having to think directly about their own feelings just yet.

There are no right and wrong labels; take the opportunity to assess your learners' abilities to link stylised features and face colours to an emotion. If learners are struggling to identify emotions at this point, then work at the basic level tasks (see Differentiation and development).

If the group are able to identify a range of emotions from the pictures – angry, worried, embarrassed, content, jealous, happy, sleepy, sad – look at the sample scenarios one at a time and discuss how each of the characters in the pictures might be feeling. Learners can either write an emotion in the thought bubble or copy a picture emotion.

Acknowledge that one situation (e.g. job interview) may make someone feel excited or another person feel nervous, or an argument may make one person worried and another angry.

Discuss everyone's individual feelings associated with the scenarios. How does each feeling look? What colour is it? What face does it have? Use the 'Choose a feeling' sheet to help generate ideas.

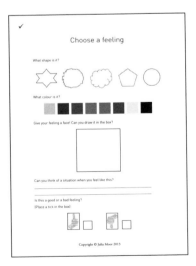

Now ask learners to choose and draw one feeling using the 'Choose a feeling' guide.

Students may wish to use the feelings prompt sheet for ideas or you may wish to describe an imaginary scenario. Ask students to volunteer to present their 'feeling' to the group. How does it look as a picture? How does it feel in your head and the rest of your body? Colour the feeling on the body printout alongside the four suggestions.

Can fellow students identify with the pictures of each other's feelings? Can learners suggest a situation when this feeling may occur?

Differentiation and development

- Students working at a higher level of emotional cognition can be encouraged to take discussion deeper using the 'change my feeling' mind maps. Talk through the mind maps and ask students to expand the boxes with their own ideas. Encourage them to identify activities and support in their own lives that they can turn to.

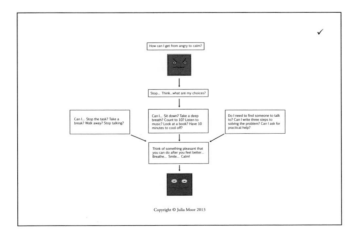

- Increase awareness that although feelings sometimes seem out of control, we can make choices to change them. Ultimately, feelings are just 'brain chemical' reactions that change and fluctuate with the things going on around us and the thoughts going on in our heads. We can choose to change our behaviours and responses but before we can do that we need to work out how to get calm, and the best way to do that is to…breathe.

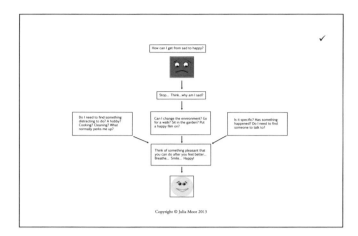

- Talk learners through ten deep slow breaths, counting 5 seconds in, 3 seconds hold and 5 seconds out. Ask them to practise this when they feel they need to take emotional control.

- To illustrate the fluctuating nature of emotions, students may draw a different emotional response in each segment of the spiral. This could be a simple line drawing, a coloured feeling picture using the 'Choose a feeling' sheet as a guide, or simply colour a range of segments from angry (red) to calm (blue). Encourage students to use the spiral as a visual reminder that all emotional states change; if they feel bad…it will pass. If they feel happy it too will pass, so enjoy the moment as it happens!

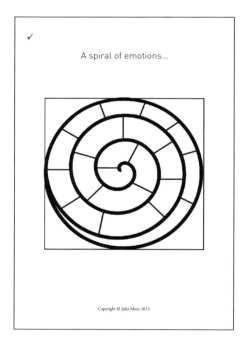

- For an easier activity you could duplicate the 'picture feelings' sheets and use them to play a matching game. Print colour versions of the sheets from the CD, copy multiple versions, cut them out and match colour to colour, and black and white images to colour. Encourage learners to also be aware of the facial expressions rather than focusing only on colours.

- You might choose to print several sets of the bigger-size images for small groups of learners to play 'emotions snap'. Again, you might print in colour from the CD if you feel the extra colour clue is required, or you could use black and white versions if not.

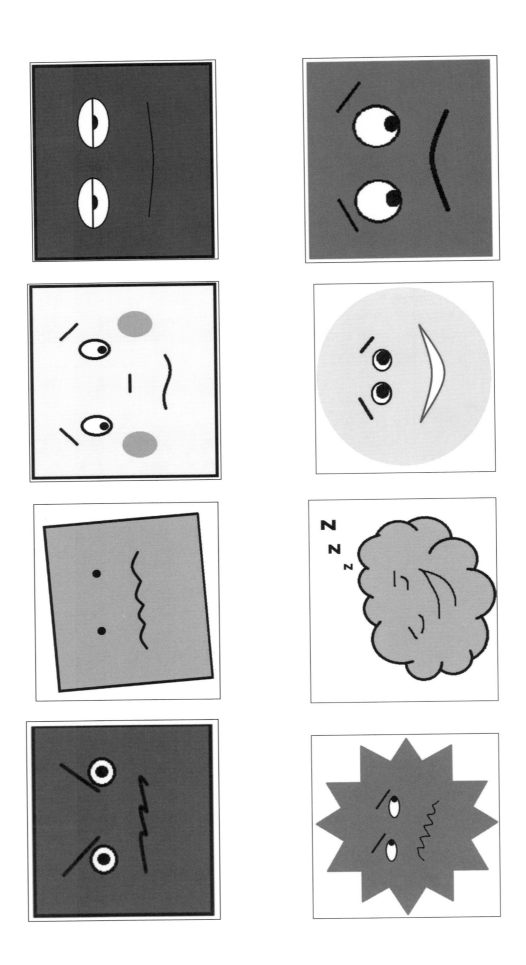

How is each person feeing in these scenes?
Write, draw or cut and paste a feeling picture in the thought bubbles.

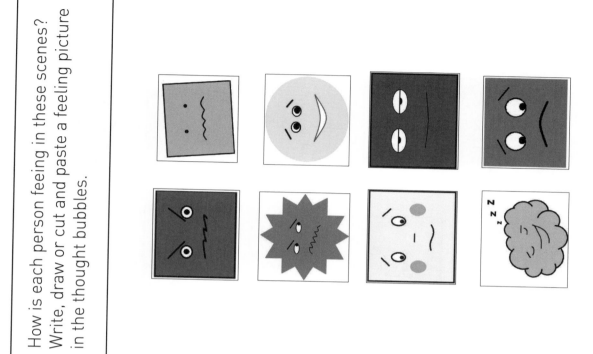

How is each person feeing in these scenes?
Write, draw or cut and paste a feeling picture in the thought bubbles.

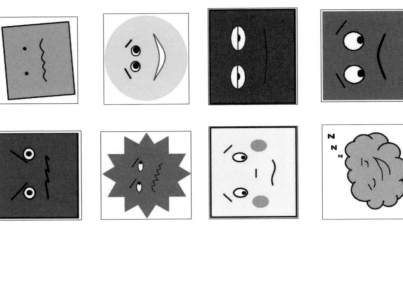

feelings

emotions

hurt jealous content

proud excited bored

happy

sad Anger sleepy Calm

Choose a feeling

What shape is it?

What colour is it?

Give your feeling a face! Can you draw it in the box?

Can you think of a situation when you feel like this?

_____

_____

Is this a good or a bad feeling?

(Place a tick in the box)

Draw a line to where you might feel the following emotions in your body.

Stress

Happiness

Excitement

Fear

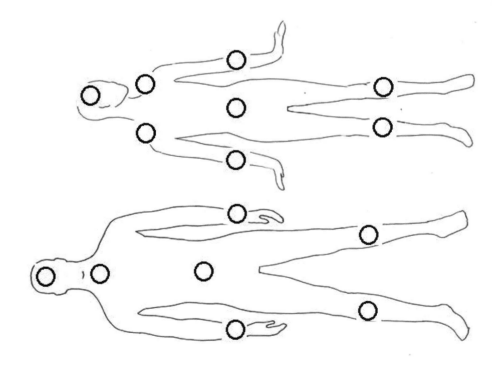

How can I get from angry to calm?

Stop... Think...what are my choices?

Can I... Sit down? Take a deep breath? Count to 10? Listen to music? Look at a book? Have 10 minutes to cool off?

Do I need to find someone to talk to? Can I write three steps to solving the problem? Can I ask for practical help?

Think of something pleasant that you can do after you feel better... Breathe... Smile... Calm!

Can I... Stop the task? Take a break? Walk away? Stop talking?

How can I get from sad to happy?

Stop... Think...why am I sad?

Is it specific? Has something happened? Do I need to find someone to talk to?

Can I change the environment? Go for a walk? Sit in the garden? Put a happy film on?

Do I need to find something distracting to do? A hobby? Cooking? Cleaning? What normally perks me up?

Think of something pleasant that you can do after you feel better... Breathe... Smile... Happy!

A spiral of emotions...

3.4 Self-Awareness
Understanding Me – Outside In

Adults living in social care are vulnerable to losing the opportunities for individual expression and being treated as unique. They can become part of a whole – a collective of 'cared-for adults' – and lose sight of their own role in maintaining and being proud of their own unique selves. Developing a strong awareness of both strengths and limitations and being able to compartmentalise disabilities, as only one aspect of who they are and not a defining label, allows people to make choices that are right for them and build on their own strengths.

Aims

- Increase awareness of others' external and internal features.
- Increase awareness of own internal and external features.
- Create an opportunity to identify areas for personal development.
- Develop an awareness of the link between self-knowledge and positive choices.
- Create the opportunity to identify support strategies.

Resources

- Printed visual guides.
- Paints/coloured pencils.
- Brushes and pens.
- White paper and card.

Prior to the activity

- Print off a set of visual guides for portrait making as follows (one set per student).

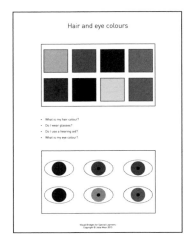

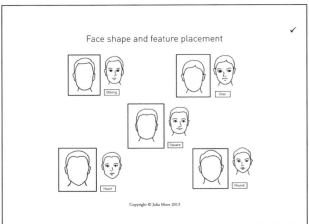

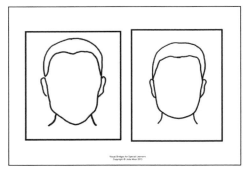

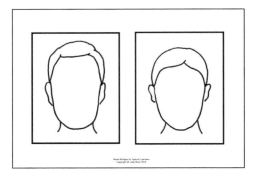

- For 'The internal me' activity, you will also need a set of the following printouts.

Delivering the activity

The complex nature of understanding own internal states means you are likely to be faced by a spectrum of abilities when introducing this topic to group learning. Before delivering the differentiated activities you will need to gauge the level of self-awareness with the individuals in the group through discussion and observation.

Lead a discussion about how we see ourselves… How we are similar to each other? More importantly, how are we all different? Explain to students that everyone is good at something and that they are going to identify the things they are good at. Explain that everyone also has areas that they may feel weaker in, things we are not so good at, and we will look at these too. When we are aware of what we are capable of and what we need support with, then we can make the right choices for all sorts of decisions. Making choices based on our strengths means we are more likely to succeed, whether that is in our choice of friends, leisure activities or work.

Ask the group what they think makes us individual.

How do we know that John is John?

Solicit answers from the group; for example, because he looks like John, he talks like John, etc.

THE PHYSICAL ME – WHAT I LOOK LIKE AND HOW OTHERS SEE ME

Guide students to examine their own and each other's facial appearance – this is a good session to follow on from Activity 3.1.

Ask students to look at their own face shape first in a handheld mirror and, using the printed visual prompts, decide what their own face shape is: oval/square/heart/round/oblong. Look at hairstyle and colour and eyes.

Provide students with paint or coloured pencils in a variety of 'skin tones' (skin tones are made of white/yellow and red in differing proportions), and the first set of visual aids. Ask students to complete a self-portrait first and then a portrait of the person sitting next to them. Remind the group that this is not an exercise to judge their art ability but to get them to really look at and study faces. Does everyone's interpretation look the same? If not then why might that be? Is it possible that if others see us differently physically to how we see ourselves, then they may also notice things about our personalities that we may not be aware of?

THE INTERNAL ME – THINGS I AM GOOD AT AND THINGS I NEED SUPPORT WITH

Take a look at James, Pete and Kim – hand each student a copy of the printouts, read out and discuss as a group.

One character at a time, ask students to list the strong points and development points (not so strong) for each character. Allow time for students to complete this individually and then bring the group back together to discuss their results.

Learners requiring some literacy clues may also wish to use the suggestions list either for spelling support or to cut and stick.

After discussing James, Pete and Kim, ask students to think now about their own strong and not so strong points. Explain that we can use the word 'development' instead of 'not so strong', as everyone can improve the things they don't feel so good at by asking for, or choosing the right support. Have a look at the suggestions on the strategy sheet and complete the thought bubbles, 'My strong points'. Ask the group to think about their 'strengths' or they may want to think about someone else's strengths in the group. These don't have to be big things, and students may need reminding that something small like 'being able to listen ' or ' smiling' or 'always being honest' are strengths. Having completed the thought bubbles, 'My strong points', compare ideas. Have students noticed strengths in each other that they haven't noticed in themselves?, for example, 'I noticed that Susan always warmly welcomes new students.'

Now move on to development points ('My not so strong points') and strategies for self-support. Do students have their own strategies and ideas? Some students will not be able to identify or recognise development areas in themselves, if this is the case, concentrate on looking at the cases of James, Pete and Kim and on identifying personality traits (see Differentiation and development). Sensitive recognition and support is required from the session leader for this aspect of the activity. Development points should always be recognised and generated by the student in order to uphold the value of the task and support self-esteem.

Differentiation and development

- For students not working at a level of internal personal awareness, concentrate on physical identity and awareness – develop self-portraits in a variety of ways.

  - You may wish to link the portraits to further work from the activities in Activity 3.1.

  - You may wish to ask learners to create several self-portraits of them portraying different feelings, either drawn or photographic.

  - You may wish to take the opportunity to work creatively using photography by creating a pencil outline from a colour portrait photo (there are many free programs on the internet that will do this) that students can then complete in a variety of media.

  ○ You may wish to develop photographic work creatively by cross-referencing to the ideas for the activities in Activity 2.7 (see Differentiation and development).

• Students working on personal development may be able to use the ideas from the activities in Activity 3.5 to set themselves specific personal development goals such as: identify the steps they could take to increase their confidence in talking to a group. Goals could be ones that make full use of strong points or could be development goals to improve not so strong points.

• Students struggling with identifying and labelling personality traits could complete flash card strips by selecting a descriptive strip and choosing a matching personality quality to write on the reverse.

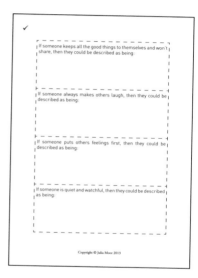 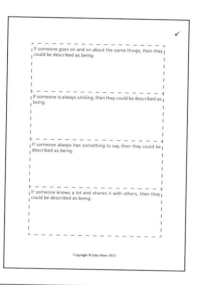 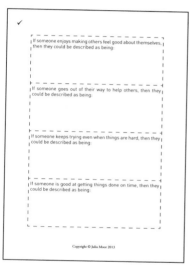

• All the personal development resources can be Braille labelled for visually impaired Braille users.

Face shape and feature placement

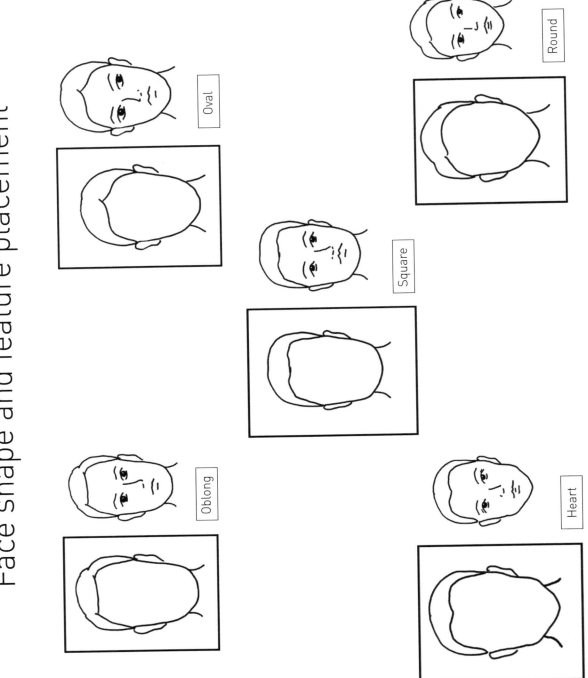

Oval

Round

Square

Oblong

Heart

This is James...

James likes his own company, he moves slowly, takes his time on tasks and likes to be accurate. Other people sometimes say he can be stubborn as James likes to do things 'his way'. James enjoys a challenge and although he can get nervous around new situations he will always 'have a go'. People tell James he's very, very good at constructing things and categorising things but although James knows he enjoys this he's not that confident at knowing how good he is. James isn't too happy in busy noisy environments where he can't concentrate.

Things James is good at: his **strong points**	Things James finds difficult: his **not so strong points**

This is Pete...

Pete is James's twin brother; they look very alike but are quite different personalities. Pete loves being around other people and is very sociable. Pete likes lots of attention and easily gets bored. He enjoys variety and loves tackling new things, though sometimes he needs to be reminded to slow down. Pete is great at cheering people up, he tells jokes and gets people smiling, though it does mean he isn't always concentrating when he is given instructions.

Things Pete is good at: his **strong points**	Things Pete finds difficult: his **not so strong points**

This is Kim...

Kim is Pete and James' friend; she gets on with all sorts of people and is a good listener. Kim enjoys good humour and likes being around people, she prefers to let others talk first and can appear a little quiet. When she's on her own Kim worries her disability holds her back and sometimes feels she can't do things as well as other people. Kim loves baking but doesn't believe her friends when they say her cakes are fantastic, she gets embarrassed and feels awkward if people compliment her.

Things Kim is good at: her **strong points**	Things Kim finds difficult: her **not so strong points**

✓

stubborn

demanding

charming

confident

loner

self starter

careful

accurate

shy

easily distracted

disciplined

quiet

fast

methodical

enthusiastic

funny

sociable

logical

My strong points

My not so strong points

Strong points	Not so strong points
• Persistence	• Give up easily
• Sociable	• Low confidence
• Accurate	• Poor time keeper
• Flexible	• Low concentration threshold
• Good concentration	• Not accurate; slap-dash
• Time keeper	• Stubborn
• Positive mental attitude	• Easily stressed
• Offers friendship and support to others	• Easily confused and muddled
• Organiser	• Not good with noise
• Self-directed	• Not good at asking for help
• Uses initiative	
• Good at working on their own	

Strategies to self-support not so strong points

- Choose tasks that feel 'doable'.
- Find strategies – picture supports/timers to help with scheduling and keeping good time.
- Find support to help schedule large tasks into a series of smaller ones and tick them off as you do them.
- Allocate an agreed amount of time for each task and try to use it.
- If you struggle to understand a different way of doing things, ask for a demonstration.
- Take time out to breathe deeply, gather thoughts and de-stress. Find something which works for you (e.g. 10 minutes of music on headphones or a walk outside). Agree a break pattern which works with those around you.
- Ask for support in the form of pictures to help with instructions.
- Choose quiet environments if noise is a problem or use ear defenders.
- Ask for support to make an 'I need help with something' card.

✓

If someone keeps all the good things to themselves and won't share, then they could be described as being:

If someone always makes others laugh, then they could be described as being:

If someone puts others feelings first, then they could be described as being:

If someone is quiet and watchful, then they could be described as being:

If someone goes on and on about the same things, then they could be described as being:

If someone is always smiling, then they could be described as being:

If someone always has something to say, then they could be described as being:

If someone knows a lot and shares it with others, then they could be described as being:

If someone enjoys making others feel good about themselves, then they could be described as being:

If someone goes out of their way to help others, then they could be described as being:

If someone keeps trying even when things are hard, then they could be described as being:

If someone is good at getting things done on time, then they could be described as being:

If someone is good at making things, then they could be described as being:

If someone is good at fixing things, then they could be described as being:

If someone is good at mixing with new people, then they could be described as being:

If someone doesn't care about others feelings, then they could be described as being:

✓

Considerate

Kind

Selfish

Persistent

Funny

Productive

Thoughtful

Generous

Disciplined

Happy

Boring

Practical

Chatty

Sociable

Knowledgeable

Mean

3.5 Self-Awareness
A Visual Strategy for Personal Goal-Setting

Identifying and setting realistic goals across many domains is a life skill that can furnish adults with the tools to make improvements in anything from learning a new hobby to improving relationships and taking charge of finances. I often find my learners either wait for others to identify goals or are quickly disappointed by not being able to achieve either an unrealistic goal or a realistic goal in an unrealistic timescale. Once a goal is identified, learners may struggle to find a strategy to break it into steps and represent this in a format that makes sense. The picture representation is a way both to organise and motivate, as well as being a visual reminder and reference, especially for goals which may involve several stages.

Aims

- Develop the ability to recognise a realistic goal.

- Develop the ability to discriminate between short-term and long-term goals.

- Develop a strategy to break goals into stages of achievement.

- Create an opportunity to identify and structure individual goals.

- Create an opportunity to recognise the work involved in achieving own goal.

Resources

- A print of the sheet 'Realistic dreams and realistic timescales?' for each student.

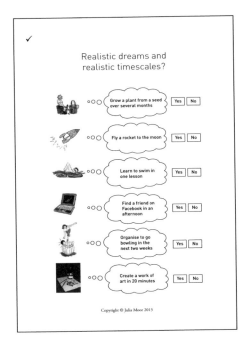

- A print of worksheet 'Minutes or weeks?' for each student.

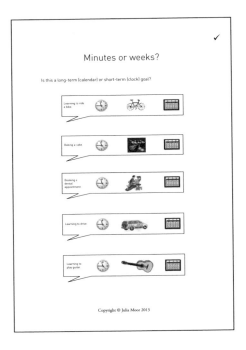

- A print of the blank flower visual (either A4 or the larger version from the CD) for each student.

- One copy of the sample visual about learning to swim for discussion.

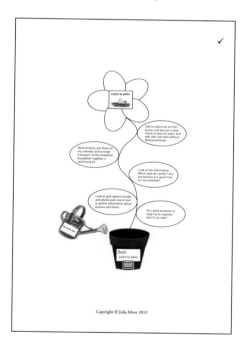

- Extra leaves and timescale indicators.

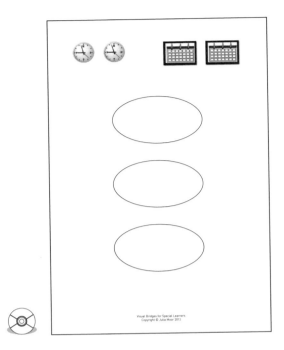

- Pens, scissors and sticky tape.

- Gather resources for Differentiation and development if required, as detailed below (e.g. photos/clip art/picture references/real flowers).

Prior to the activity

Print off the materials. If you are using the large-size flower visuals, assemble them by by taping the sheets together.

Delivering the activity

Discuss what a goal is with examples. Use personal and fictitious examples to get the group talking about goals they have both achieved in the past or want to in the future. Students may also wish to identify goals they may have for a particular course. Discuss any failed ambitions and reasons why these weren't achieved. Remind the group that goals don't have to be big; we can get a sense of independence and achievement from anything we don't normally do but want to accomplish. Ask the group for suggestions of such goals, for example 'learn to set the recorder for the TV' or 'bake a cake independently'.

Discuss what a realistic goal is and what realistic timeframes are, using the 'Realistic dreams and realistic timescales?' worksheet. Learners could complete these individually or as a group discussion exercise.

Some of the goals on the sheet are long term (e.g. learning to swim/growing a plant) and some are short term (e.g. find a friend on a social network).

We can use the clock symbol for short-term goals – it will take minutes or hours.

Use the calendar symbol for long-term goals – it will take days or weeks.

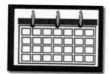

Look at the 'Minutes or weeks?' worksheet and ask students to decide how long each goal might take by joining the picture to the clock or calendar symbol with a line.

Talk about how all goals, both long term and short term, can be broken down into the stages required to complete them.

We can make this easier to see by making them into a picture. Hand out a copy of the sample flower visual for learning to swim and talk through the stages involved.

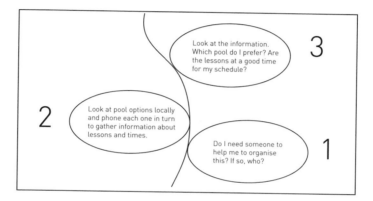

Discuss the symbolism of the flower – it takes a while to grow, one leaf at a time before it reaches its final goal and flowers. On the way, it needs nurturing through practice by ourselves and maybe support from someone we have identified and asked. Some flowers may only have three or four leaves; some may need lots before they bloom.

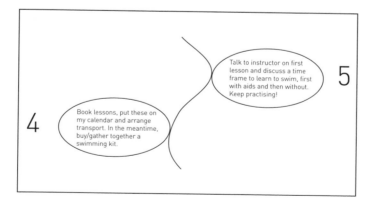

Another person learning to swim may add a leaf for 'take first level badge' or 'arrange for family to watch me for encouragement' or 'put face in water'.

Now ask learners to think about a personal goal of their own. For the time being this is just an exercise to show students how they can go about structuring the tasks involved in achieving something, so remind learners that this is not necessarily something they have to commit to right now (though, all being well, some students will be motivated to do just that!).

Remind learners this could be a practical goal such as 'learn to knit' or a personal development goal such as 'become more confident at shopping on my own' or a course related goal such as 'complete initial ideas board in three weeks' or 'learn to use a search engine in three sessions'.

When students have a goal in mind, supply them with the visual to complete collaboratively with the teacher by breaking the goal into five or more steps. Remind students that they may add extra steps if they wish and should add a timescale indicator.

Students will write or draw their goal and timescale on the pot. They will also identify (if required) the name of someone who can support or mentor them with this goal and write this on the watering can.

Talk students through the stages either as a group or individually.

- Do I need help and who will help me?

- What equipment do I need?

- How long will I allow myself to complete this – is it a short-term or long-term goal?

- When and where will I work on my goal?

Allow time for students to talk to each other and for any support available to them about their goals and to gain feedback. If they want to tackle the identified goal they have just worked on, then all they need do is refer to each leaf one at a time, complete and tick it off.

Some students may wish to take a blank visual to complete later.

Differentiation and development

- The flower visual can be completed on a single A4 sheet or on four A4 sheets taped together, depending on student preferences. Some students may wish to represent each stage using pictures (drawn or clip art) or photos and will need the larger version. They may wish to add photos as they progress or add notes.

- Braille users could complete the visual using Braille stages on a raised cut-out flower.

- Perhaps handle real flowers at the start of the session for a multi-sensory experience and to remind students about the structure of the flower and its symbolism.

- The exercise can be used at a very basic level from identifying the stages involved in accomplishing a simple task to the personal goal setting described here, to long-term life goals such as living independently or securing employment.

- Remember to print off some visual material (from internet images or clip art) for the students working at a level of sequencing stages. Some suggestions might be the sequence of steps in:

  - making a cup of tea or a sandwich

  - getting ready to go out for a walk

  - going to the cinema.

The scope for the development of this activity is as broad as the individuals' motivation and imagination. Encourage students working on goals to keep returning to their visual to see where they are at in their progress, to add notes and stages if necessary and to keep on track.

Students may want to write how they feel when they have achieved their goals on each of the petals, for example safe, proud, healthy, confident, happy.

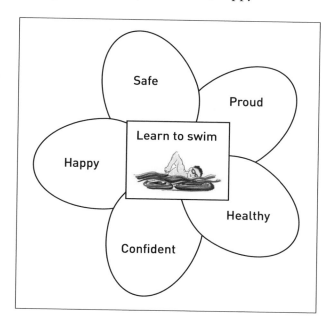

Realistic dreams and realistic timescales?

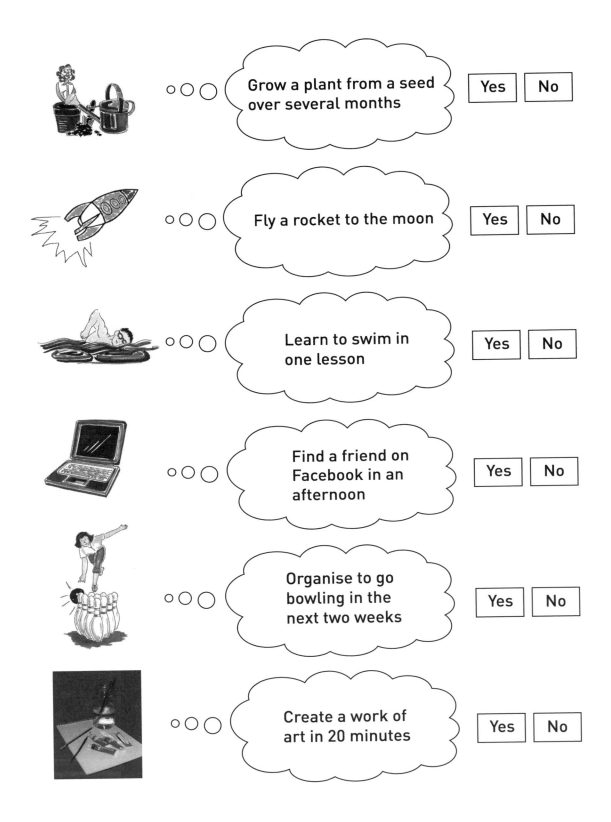

Grow a plant from a seed over several months — Yes | No

Fly a rocket to the moon — Yes | No

Learn to swim in one lesson — Yes | No

Find a friend on Facebook in an afternoon — Yes | No

Organise to go bowling in the next two weeks — Yes | No

Create a work of art in 20 minutes — Yes | No

Minutes or weeks?

Is this a long-term (calendar) or short-term (clock) goal?

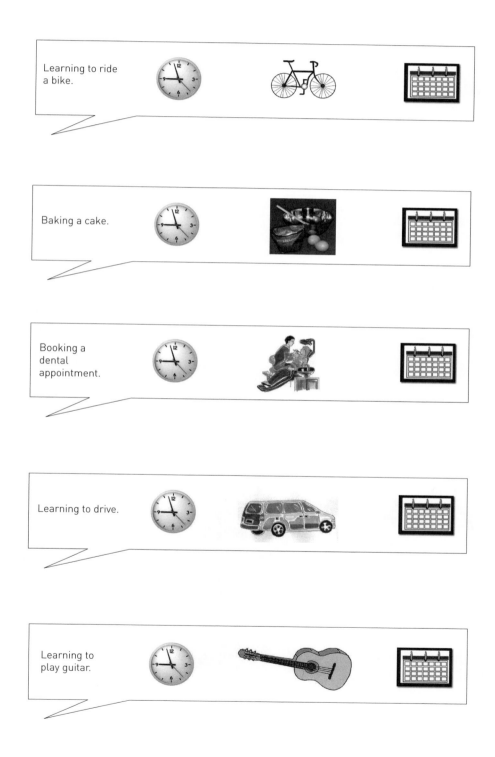

Learning to ride a bike.

Baking a cake.

Booking a dental appointment.

Learning to drive.

Learning to play guitar.

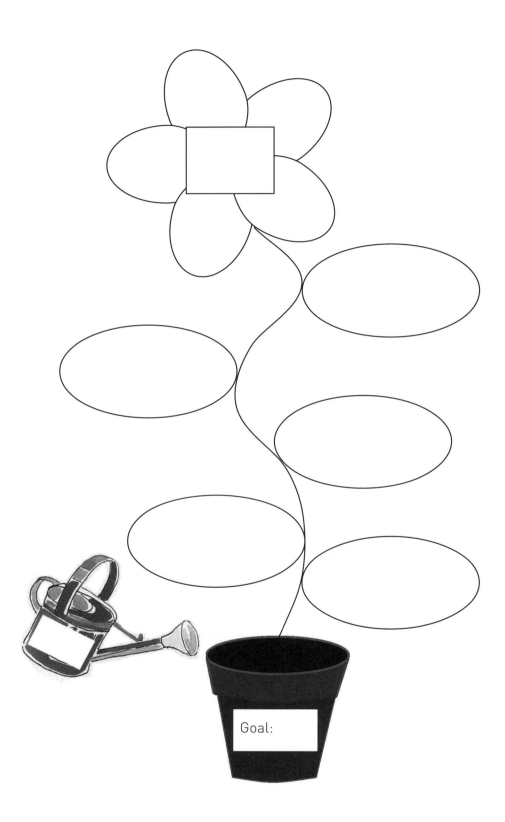

Goal:

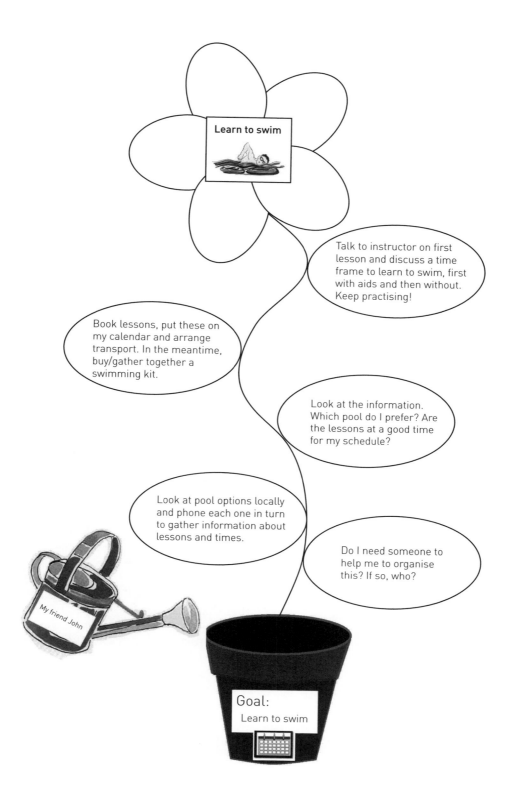

Learn to swim

Talk to instructor on first lesson and discuss a time frame to learn to swim, first with aids and then without. Keep practising!

Book lessons, put these on my calendar and arrange transport. In the meantime, buy/gather together a swimming kit.

Look at the information. Which pool do I prefer? Are the lessons at a good time for my schedule?

Look at pool options locally and phone each one in turn to gather information about lessons and times.

Do I need someone to help me to organise this? If so, who?

My friend John

Goal:
Learn to swim

3.6 Awareness of Others
Using Preference Portraits
to Get to Know Others

This activity is a natural follow on from Activity 3.2 and enables learners to look at and assess the preferences of others by identifying differences and similarities and using the Picture Preference Portrait as a communication aid. I find this activity supports students to start conversations by directing their questions to positive preferences. Most people enjoy communicating about themselves. This activity enables students to do just that and also to practise asking questions and taking an interest in others.

Aims

- Develop awareness of the preferences of others members of the group.

- Develop skills in interpreting picture information.

- Practise identifying trends, differences and similarities by gathering simple data.

- Create an opportunity to verbally address a group.

- Create an opportunity to develop conversation topics with peers.

Resources

- Each student will have already completed their own Picture Preference Portrait – you may wish to hand copies of these out (rather than originals).

- A copy of 'Identifying trends, differences and similarities' for each student.

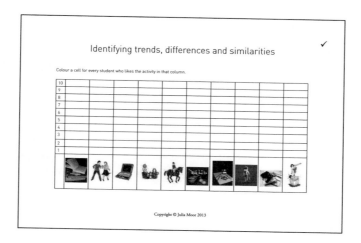

- Coloured pens.

- A copy of the mind map 'Finding out more about my partner's likes' for each student.

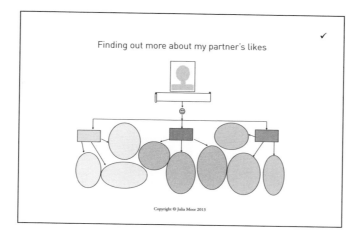

Delivering the activity

Students should be familiar with the Picture Preference Portrait having already completed their own. Ask the group for consent to share their portraits with each other, explaining why it is a positive thing to try to understand everyone else's likes and dislikes, that is:

- to help with smooth relationships

- to give us conversation clues

- to better understand why someone may behave a certain way.

Allow learners several minutes to exchange and look at each other's portraits and process the information on them. Using the portraits encourage students to spend five minutes talking to each other to clarify what their portrait says about them.

One at a time, ask learners to introduce the person they are sat next to by using the portraits: 'This is…, he likes…', etc. Include any extra information that may have been gathered and identify one thing that this portrait has in common with their own.

Now ask learners to look at their group as a whole and build up a picture of likes and dislikes using the simple bar chart ('Identifying trends, differences and similarities'). Task each student to gather information on one column only and complete a bar for that column by taking turns to ask the group for a show of hands. Look at the results together, finding people with similar likes. Which is the most popular activity and the least popular? Which activities are popular but not on the bar chart?

Now that the students have got to know a little about each other and their commonalities as a group, using the same portrait they have introduced learners can now go on to research more about their partner's likes. Starting with three of their preferences on the portrait, allow students time to gain more information. For example, if they say they like TV, art and cooking, students could ask for three more pieces of information about each of these topics. For example, which programmes do you like? How much TV do you watch a day? Do you plan what to watch or just switch it on? Or for Art... What medium do you like to work with? Do you take classes? What subjects do you like to draw? And so on...

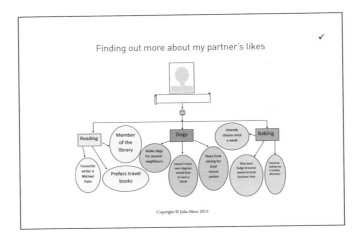

Regroup and talk about the results. Did students find it easy or difficult? Did the Picture Preference Portrait give them a starting point? Did they feel that once conversation got going on someone's favourite subject then they really opened up and started talking? Remind learners that it's easier to start a conversation with someone if you ask them questions about something you already know they are interested in or, better still, something that you both have in common and enjoy. Don't forget to return the mind maps and portraits back to their owners.

Differentiation and development

- The activity 'Finding out more about my partner's likes' does demand a higher level of language and communication ability than the data-gathering exercise. For students struggling with this level of language you may wish to provide the portrait print from Activity 3.4, which concentrates on examining someone else's external physical features.

- The natural development to this activity is to move on to Activity 3.7 and Activity 3.8. Both these activities help to develop understanding of more complex internal states.

Identifying trends, differences and similarities

Colour a cell for every student who likes the activity in that column.

10	9	8	7	6	5	4	3	2	1	

Finding out more about my partner's likes

Finding out more about my partner's likes

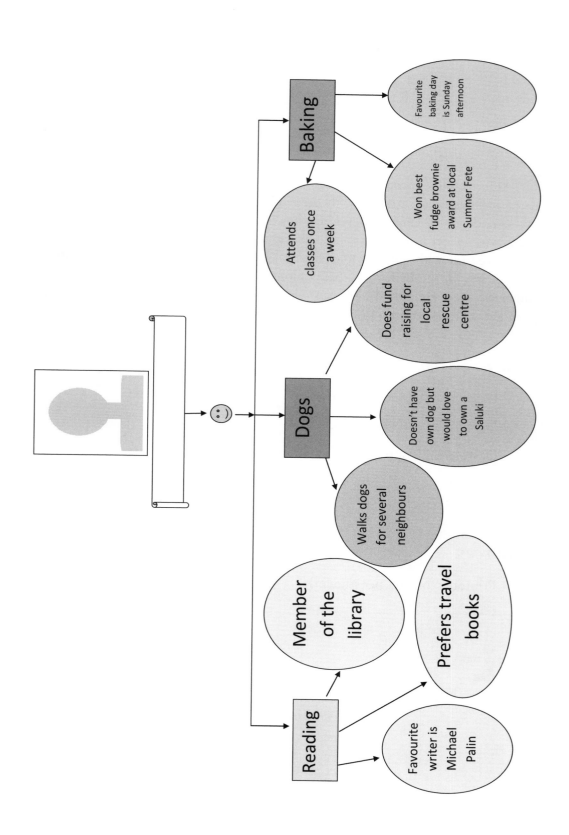

Baking
- Favourite baking day is Sunday afternoon
- Won best fudge brownie award at local Summer Fete
- Attends classes once a week

Dogs
- Does fund raising for local rescue centre
- Doesn't have own dog but would love to own a Saluki
- Walks dogs for several neighbours

Reading
- Member of the library
- Prefers travel books
- Favourite writer is Michael Palin

3.7 Awareness of Others
Situations, Feelings, Actions

This session builds on and extends the activities in Activity 3.3 to developing awareness of others' feelings by identifying with their dilemmas. Learners engaging with this activity will have a good general language level but may be struggling with identifying causal links between others' internal emotional states and behaviours. Many of my learners share homes, workplaces and leisure time with other people who may have difficulties in processing, communication or learning. For all the benefits of being alongside others in life that are coping with the same challenges, there are also the stresses and tensions that problems understanding each other's personal circumstances can bring.

Aims

- Develop awareness and understanding of others' mind states.

- Develop imagination skills.

- Develop skills at observation and interpretation.

- Create the opportunity to use a strategy to understand others' actions and the feelings behind them.

Resources

- Printouts (one set per student):

- A copy of 'What is James confused about…?' to pass amongst students.

- Pens.

Prior to the activity

- Gather together the printed materials, including the 'scaled-down' version for differentiation if required (see Differentiation and development).

Delivering the activity

Start the activity by asking the group why it is a good thing to try to understand how others are feeling – how does this benefit us? This sounds like a simple question but many of my students tackle tensions, misunderstandings and relationship difficulties by looking at how others are behaving towards them without fully understanding the role of their own behaviour. By facilitating a discussion around our personal behaviour towards others, learners can be enabled to view a situation more objectively. Suggest to the group that the following positives can happen when we are more aware of what might be going on in others' heads:

- We can build stronger friendships.

- We can avoid unnecessary stress and tension.

- We can anticipate reactions and try to avoid negative triggers.

We need to be able to observe and build theories in order to understand what is going on in others' heads. Use the example of James…

Pass the 'What is James confused about…?' worksheet around the group. Can the group work out his dilemma just from the picture?

Lead a discussion with the group about how we can assess a situation quickly just by watching what is happening… How does James look? Calm? Angry? Stressed?

Of course it would be great if everyone carried a thought bubble that we could also see! If we were really with James at this time, we would also have to hear what he has to say; for example, 'Oh no, I've just taken an order off that table and I can't remember what drinks they've ordered – I know there are some coffees and a tea, but I don't know who has sugar or milk and who ordered what!' We would then be able to explain why he looked so worried. If we were in a position to help James we could do something…we could act. For example, we could suggest that James goes back to the table with a notebook and, after apologising, takes the order again. Or we may suggest James just takes the milk in a jug and sugar in a bowl for the customers to help themselves. If James is looking stressed, we could offer to help make one of the drinks. Finally, we might have to accept that it could take James a little time to feel back on top of things and allow him to concentrate quietly before we redirect his attention.

Explain to the group that we could do all these things every time we judge a situation we are unsure of – we can…**Watch**, **Hear**, **Explain**, **Act** and allow **Time**.

Pass students the 'WHEAT' handout and talk them through it. Then allow time to complete the 'Reassure!' sheet as an individual activity.

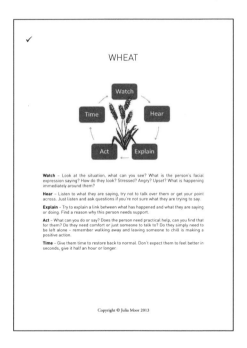

Evaluate the activity together and then move on to 'Making someone new feel at home', 'Saying sorry…' and 'Comfort'. Using the 'WHEAT' cue sheet, ask students to complete the exercises and share their suggestions with the rest of the group.

Differentiation and development

- The activity can be scaled down by just presenting students with the picture sheet and soliciting suggestions for what might be happening in each picture. Who could be saying what? How might they be feeling?

- Students may wish to go on to identify social encounters in their own lives that have happened in the past or may potentially happen and revisit how they might respond in the situation now using the 'WHEAT' prompts.

WHEAT

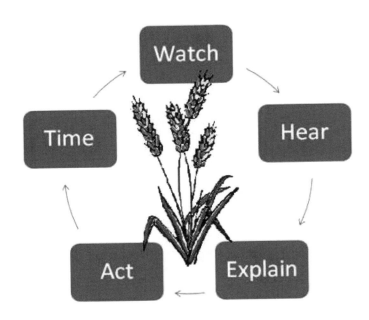

Watch – Look at the situation, what can you see? What is the person's facial expression saying? How do they look? Stressed? Angry? Upset? What is happening immediately around them?

Hear – Listen to what they are saying, try not to talk over them or get your point across. Just listen and ask questions if you're not sure what they are trying to say.

Explain – Try to explain a link between what has happened and what they are saying or doing. Find a reason why this person needs support.

Act – What can you do or say? Does the person need practical help, can you find that for them? Do they need comfort or just someone to talk to? Do they simply need to be left alone – remember walking away and leaving someone to chill is making a positive action.

Time – Give them time to restore back to normal. Don't expect them to feel better in seconds, give it half an hour or longer.

Making someone new feel at home

Colin has just been introduced to Sarah. Sarah has joined his college course for the first time and feels a little overwhelmed and scared.

Think about **WHEAT**...

Watch... What can you see? Who is looking scared?

_____

_____

_____

Hear... What is Colin saying?

_____

_____

_____

What is Sarah saying?

_____

_____

Explain... Why is Sarah feeling scared?

_____

_____

Act... Could Colin say or do something to help the situation?

_____

_____

Time... Does Sarah need time to feel more confident?

_____

_____

What could Colin say to Sarah to make her feel at home? Fill in the speech bubble.

Saying sorry...

Jonathon is angry with Steven. Steven forgot to record his favourite TV programme despite being asked to do so on a number of occasions. Jonathon has always helped Steven and done small favours for him, so he feels let down and fed up.

Think about **WHEAT**...

Watch... What can you see? Who is angry?

_____

_____

Hear... What is Steven saying?

_____

_____

What is Jonathon saying?

_____

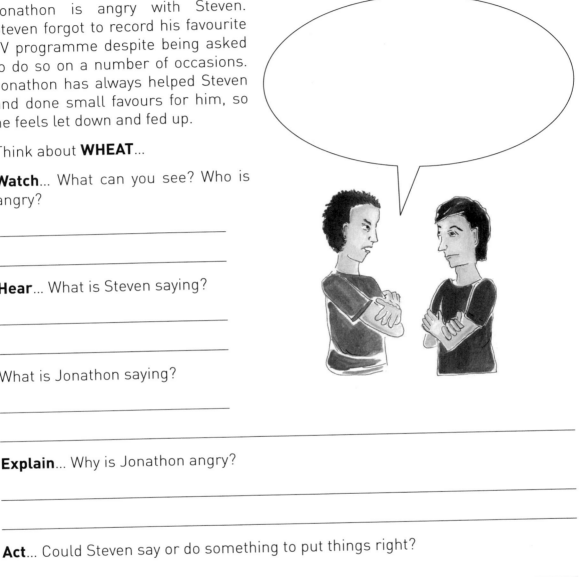

Explain... Why is Jonathon angry?

_____

_____

Act... Could Steven say or do something to put things right?

_____

_____

Time... Does Jonathon need Steven to give him time?

_____

_____

What can Steven say to let Jonathon know he is genuinely sorry and will promise not to let him down again? Fill in the speech bubble.

Reassure!

James has started work in a café and has been given instructions to hand out 2 coffees and 1 tea. He can't remember who has coffee or tea and who has sugar or not. He gets cross and confused and is embarrassed that he's struggling with what appears to be a simple job.

Think about **WHEAT**...

Watch... What can you see?

_____

_____

Hear... What might James be saying?

_____

_____

Explain... Why is James confused?

_____

_____

Act... If you were helping James, what would you do?

_____

_____

Time... Does James need time?

_____

_____

What would **YOU** say to James? Fill in the speech bubble.

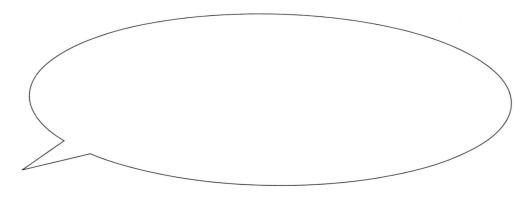

Comfort

Katy has been looking forward to her holiday with her friend Sandra for months. She was so excited and happy, the sun was shining and her bags were packed. Katy has now just had a phone call to say the holiday has been cancelled because Sandra has broken her wrist. Katy is desperately disappointed and sad.

Think about **WHEAT**...

Watch... What can you see?

_____

_____

Hear... What might Katy be saying?

_____

_____

Explain... Why is Katy sad?

_____

_____

Act... If you were helping Katy, what would you do?

_____

_____

Time... Does Katy need time?

_____

_____

What would **YOU** say to Katy? Fill in the speech bubble.

What is James confused about...?

What are we feeling? What could we be thinking? What could we be saying?

3.8 Awareness of Others
Different Perspectives

This is a good activity to follow Activity 3.7, as it enables learners to further explore how situations and interactions can run more positively by using choice and communication. Many of my learners have difficulty predicting the thoughts and intentions of others and don't naturally learn this from emotional feedback during everyday encounters. To take an academic look at fictitious situations gives learners the chance to explore their knowledge and judgement of others and develop awareness of others through an intellectual rather than emotive route.

Aims

- Develop awareness of different viewpoints.

- Develop imagination skills to envisage a different outcome.

- Develop skills at observation and interpretation.

Resources

- A copy of the 'Different perspectives' worksheet for each student.

- A copy of each of the perspectives worksheets for each student.

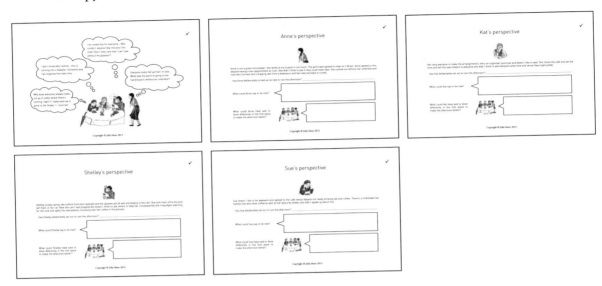

- Pens/pencils.

- 'Scaled-down' worksheet if necessary (see Differentiation and development).

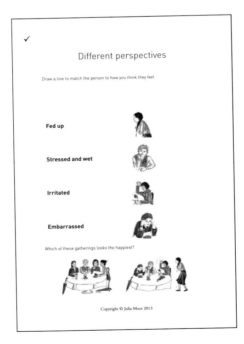

Prior to the activity

- Print off worksheets and gather resources.

Delivering the activity

Begin with a definition of perspective by asking students to describe in turn exactly what they see directly ahead of them in one word (you may wish to ask students to narrow their field of vision by placing their hands up to the sides of their eyes). Students may see another learner, an object or part of the room. Visually impaired students may wish to identify the sound closest and most prominent to them. Compare answers… Are they all the same? With any luck, everyone will have identified something slightly different. Solicit reasons why this might be and introduce the word 'perspective', that is, our very own personal view (literally in this case).

Develop the discussion of perspective to also include our very own private interpretation of events (our internal view) and demonstrate this by asking for volunteers to 'mind read' your thoughts. Tell them you are thinking really hard about a particular subject and ask them to guess what that is. Pretty difficult? However, if we give each other clues by communicating as much as we are able, then we can guess more accurately what someone is thinking. Try the 'mind reading' exercise again; tell the group you are thinking of 'a small animal, or a shape or a mode of transport' and allow the group to take turns guessing…very soon someone will get the answer right. We can communicate a clue verbally like this, or our faces and the situations we are in can give a clue to what we are thinking.

Make the activity meaningful by asking the group if they sometimes feel confused by people's actions, if they have ever upset someone but not known why or have been upset by someone else who didn't seem to be aware of it. Describe that by spending time thinking about how we can place ourselves into other's shoes (look at a situation from the other person's perspective) we can reduce negative social encounters.

Now look at the 'Different perspectives' worksheet. Spend a couple of minutes looking at the café picture and ask the students to write a thought or feeling for each character in the bubble from their own perspective, that is, their own view on the situation.

Compare everyone's ideas for each character one at a time, then as a group look at the sheet that gives everyone's perspectives (either hand a copy to share between two students or project for the class to see). Are we getting a clearer idea that everyone is feeling fed up, sad, stressed…?

Now, one by one, look at each character in detail from their own perspective.

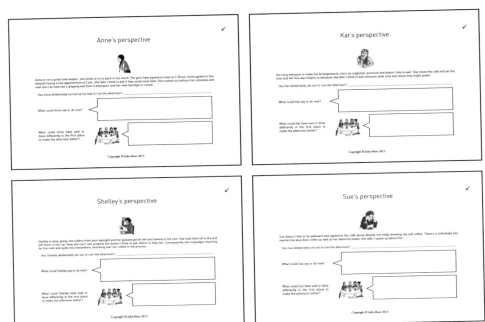

You may wish to get your students to do this in twos, work on it as a group exercise or have everyone working on a sheet individually. The worksheets describe the character in more detail. The following is an example of how Anne's perspective could be handled with the group.

Read out the scenario:

> Anne is not a great time keeper; she tends to try to pack in too much. The girls have agreed to meet at 2.30 pm. Anne agreed to this despite having a hair appointment at 2 pm. She didn't think to ask if they could meet later. She rushed out without her umbrella and now she's arrived she's dripping wet from a downpour and her new hairstyle is ruined.

Ask students to think about whether everyone has set out deliberately to make the experience negative.

- *Has Anne deliberately turned up too late to ruin the afternoon?* Students should discuss that the common answer is 'no' for all of the characters.

So at this moment she's half an hour late and wet through...

- *What could Anne say or do now?* She could probably start with an apology to her friends and just be honest about trying to fit in too much. She could try to enjoy the fact that they are altogether now and excuse herself for five minutes in the restroom to dry her hair and clothes and make the best of it.

  How might an alternative outcome have played out?…

- *What could Anne have said or done differently in the first place to make the afternoon better?* There could be several appropriate suggestions for this. She could perhaps have made her appointment for a different day or moved it forward to an earlier time. She could have set her alarm clock an hour earlier to make sure she had everything she needed and wasn't rushing. She could have asked her friends to meet at 3 pm instead of 2.30 pm.

Differentiation and development

- The session could be delivered as a group discussion activity to accommodate learners unable to engage due to literacy or visual difficulties. There is also a 'scaled-down' worksheet to allow for less language processing.

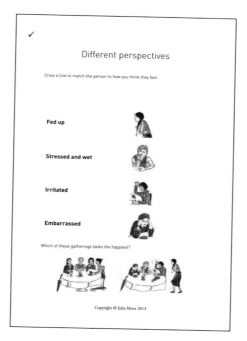

- This activity is a natural part of the full section on self-awareness and awareness of others, so lends itself well to being tied to the other activities to develop and extend social knowledge and skills over several weeks. Learning should be reinforced and embedded in the sessions by gentle questioning or generalising to the learning situation. For example, if you take a tea break in the session you may want to ask how you would ensure this went well for two more fictitious students: Shelley (watch out for those spectacles!) and Sue (has she brought her own choice of refreshment?).

Different perspectives

Anne, Kat, Shelley and Sue are all good friends. They like each other but you wouldn't think so to look at them, would you?! They don't often all get together and when they do there are problems despite the fact they all like each other. Perhaps things could be different if they could each communicate their own perspective better...

This is Anne – she's not a great time keeper and is always in a rush.

This is Kat – she's an organiser and likes people to be on time.

This is Shelley – she should wear glasses but left them in her car.

This is Sue – she doesn't like tea or coffee.

Anne's perspective

Anne is not a great time keeper; she tends to try to pack in too much. The girls have agreed to meet at 2.30 pm. Anne agreed to this despite having a hair appointment at 2 pm. She didn't think to ask if they could meet later. She rushed out without her umbrella and now she's arrived she's dripping wet from a downpour and her new hairstyle is ruined.

Has Anne deliberately turned up too late to ruin the afternoon?

What could Anne say or do now?

What could Anne have said or done differently in the first place to make the afternoon better?

Kat's perspective

Kat rang everyone to make the arrangements; she's an organiser, punctual and doesn't like to wait. She chose the café and set the time and felt this was helpful to everyone she didn't think to ask everyone what time and venue they might prefer.

Has Kat deliberately set out to ruin the afternoon? _____

What could Kat say or do now?

What could Kat have said or done differently in the first place to make the afternoon better?

Shelley's perspective

Shelley is easy-going, she suffers from poor eyesight and her glasses got all wet and steamy in the rain. She took them off to dry and left them in her car. Now she can't see properly but doesn't think to ask others to help her. Consequently she misjudges reaching for the milk and spills this everywhere, knocking over her coffee in the process.

Has Shelley deliberately set out to ruin the afternoon? _____

What could Shelley say or do now?

What could Shelley have said or done differently in the first place to make the afternoon better?

Sue's perspective

Sue doesn't like to be awkward and agreed to the café venue despite not really drinking tea and coffee. There's a milkshake bar nearby that also does coffee as well as her favourite shake, she didn't speak up about this.

Has Sue deliberately set out to ruin the afternoon?

What could Sue say or do now?

What could Sue have said or done differently in the first place to make the afternoon better?

Different perspectives

Draw a line to match the person to how you think they feel.

Fed up

Stressed and wet

Irritated

Embarrassed

Which of these gatherings looks the happiest?

SECTION 4

Exploring Representation, Language and Literacy
'The Fruit Bowl'

Introduction

Activity 4.1 Mark Making: Control Copy and Colour

Activity 4.2 Discuss and Describe: Language Development; Adjectives

Activity 4.3 Rhythm and Rhyme: Finding and Using Rhymes

Activity 4.4 Storytelling: Take a Picture, Weave a Narrative

 All photocopiable sheets that accompany these activities can also be printed in colour from the CD at the back of the book. This icon denotes any sheets that can be found on the CD, but are not included in this book.

Introduction

Adult learners with developmental disabilities often struggle to decode speech sounds, retain instructions, extract meaning, organise, plan and retrieve words, or remember what they want to say next in short-term memory. This all makes understanding *written* language seem way out of reach and teachers and carers quite appropriately may feel that other life and language skills should take precedence within a learning environment. However, if we take a broader definition of literacy as another arm of communication and representation (that a word, sound, picture or symbol can represent an action, object or feeling), then to pursue developing skills at whatever level of decoding the student is at, will add to their whole communication repertoire. For example, this might include strengthening a student's cognition that a photo represents an activity or a series of pictures represents a task sequence. It may involve practising the fine motor skills in simple mark making to colour a representation of something (e.g. a picture) or be more elaborate and precise marks that can be guided into copying letter shapes to make a word. For students already in possession of literacy skills, the activities can help develop imaginative storytelling or increase vocabulary. There are so many levels and so many activities that can be pursued to increase language cognition that I have chosen to narrow this section to one themed topic: the fruit bowl.

Why this subject? Well, on a multi-sensory level you will be able to engage your students in handling, cutting, smelling, and tasting – a highly motivating start to a communication session. Within the group I am expecting you will be trying to differentiate activities from the basic mark making to creative writing as described above; by keeping the same theme for all activities, students will be looking at their own and each other's images and listening to language that has a common theme. Students are not isolated by their ability level; they are able to engage with each other, share verbal and non-verbal reactions to exploring the same subject and feel like they are all making a contribution to the learning experience. Just as importantly, they will all be working with material that is not an adaption from primary school resources intended for very young children but with a theme and images that, although simple and accessible, also feel 'grown up'.

This section has four main activities:

- Activity 4.1 Mark Making

- Activity 4.2 Discuss and Describe

- Activity 4.3 Rhythm and Rhyme

- Activity 4.4 Storytelling

Each main activity has a minimum of two ability levels, leaving you with eight plus activities ranging through several cognitive levels all around the one theme. All the activities could be worked to a number of different themes once the fruit bowl has been exhausted and you are comfortable with the feel of delivering multiple activities tied by the same language. The most motivating activities of all will be to rework the fruit bowl concept around a subject matter each student finds personally motivating.

4.1 Mark Making
Control, Copy and Colour

Mark making in early years is an essential precursor to developing the fine motor skills required to form letter shapes. If those marks never evolve into letter shapes due to severe developmental delay, how can mark making in adult years be of benefit to the broader context of communication?

I find my adults working at a pre-literate stage enjoy the opportunity to mark make and engage with pens and paper for a variety of reasons. It enables the individual to have control over a cause–effect sequence, that is, to make a lasting mark (literally) on paper. The repetition of making a sequence of marks can often be rhythmic and relaxing and these positive sensations put learners in a context that prepares them to relate and interact. Individuals can be successful at any ability level, whether they are simply working on applying enough pressure to transfer a mark or working on more precise 'colouring' by copying an already coloured image. As a communication exercise, the shared attention to an image, either imaginary, implied or real, can draw out positive interactions from eye contact to single words to whole sentences.

Learners can, however, often get bored or demotivated just mark making for the sake of it on blank paper. By focusing an 'event' around a multi-sensory theme and having an image laid out to copy or (at a slightly higher level of pen control), connecting dots or tracing to complete an image, learners stay on task, are not left feeling they are engaging with childish images and can take their finished work as far as their ability will let them.

Aims

- Develop and practise fine motor skills.

- Strengthen finger muscles to control pressure and position.

- Create an opportunity to participate and interact with both media and people around a single theme.

- Create an opportunity to complete an artistic representation.

- Practise colour knowledge.

Resources

- Copies of the colouring pages and their completed colour images (available on the CD).

- Coloured pencils/sharpeners (you may wish to provide different widths of pencil and pencil grips to accommodate learners with physical grip difficulties).

- Masking tape to secure papers to the table if required.

- Copies of the connect the dots worksheets:

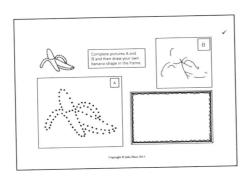 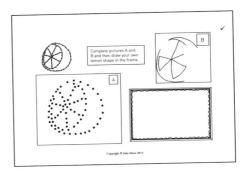

 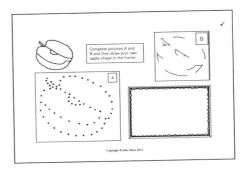

- Real fruit (banana, lemon, pineapple, apple; preferably two of each – one to study and one to taste).

- Chopping board and knife.

- Wet wipes and kitchen roll.

Prior to the activity

Gather resources and print out sheets.

How would you describe me in six words?

_____

_____

_____

_____

_____

_____

How would you describe me in six words?

_____

_____

_____

_____

_____

_____

✓

soft

white

perfumed

curved

dry

fragile

tropical

filling

bendy

✓

sharp   sour

acidic

tart

juicy

bitter   tangy

zesty

clean

✓

spiky

perfumed

sweet

yellow

juicy

hard

tropical

mouth-watering

quenching

✓

round   shiny

sweet

red   **crunchy**

sharp   **juicy**

crisp   fresh

Awesome	Beautiful	Enchanting	Immaculate	Marvellous
Acidic	Bruised	Exotic	Impeccable	Mighty
Agreeable	Bendy	Exciting	Incomparable	Moody
Amazing	Bite-sized	Edible	Ideal	Mysterious
Aromatic	Bright	Elegant	Interesting	Pimply
Odourful	Outrageous	Organic	Oval	Offensive
Pink	Prickly	Pristine	Nice	Nutritious
Lasting	Lovely	Little	Light	Loose
Natural	Necessary	Palatable		

✓

B_____

A_____

N_____

A_____

N_____

A_____

✓

L_____

E_____

M_____

O_____

N_____

P_____

I_____

N_____

E_____

A_____

P_____

P_____

L_____

E_____

A_____

P_____

P_____

L_____

E_____

4.3 Rhythm and Rhyme
Finding and Using Rhymes

Rhythm and song are intrinsic to language acquisition. We all have an instinct to rhyme, either with words or sounds, and to attend to and pick out rhyming patterns and sounds. I also find many of my learners enjoy idiosyncratic rhythmic movements and activities that may look unusual externally but hold safety, comfort and meaning for the individual. This activity again builds on the fruit bowl theme, using all the sensory exploration previously described to solicit language ideas and develop and extend vocabulary. If I presented my learners with an open task to produce a piece of rhyming poetry around a topic, many of my students would feel out of their depth and withdraw from the activity. However, if I produce a template to complete a poem, learners are challenged to find a rhyme from a selection of options which they are usually successful at. This further motivates them to offer their original ideas and makes the whole creative writing process much less daunting.

Aims

- Develop and extend descriptive language.

- Develop imagination skills.

- Create the opportunity to identify rhyming words.

- Develop awareness of rhyming and non-rhyming poetry.

- Create the opportunity for choice.

Resources

- Copy of the sample poem, 'The Fruit Bowl'.

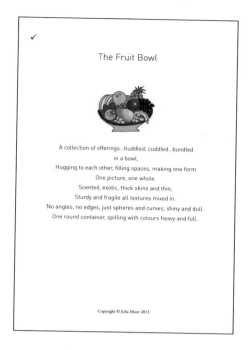

- Copies of the finding rhymes sheets, both word and picture versions (see Differentiation and development).

- Copies of each of the poetry templates.

- Pens, pencils, and any other items required (see Differentiation and development).

- Real fruit (banana, lemon, pineapple, apple), chopping board, knife, paper towel, wet wipes.

Prior to the activity

Assemble resources and print off worksheets.

Delivering the activity

As with all the activities in the fruit bowl sessions, begin with a general conversation about fruit as a language theme. Pass the fruit around the group to handle, smell and look at. Describe colours, textures, weight. Are the fruit shiny or dull? Are they one shade or several? Allow students plenty of time to contribute to the discussion before cutting the fruit and offering tastes. Continue to develop interactions around taste words, individual preferences and dislikes. Ask the group to be aware of rhyming words, for example sweet…heat, as they engage in their discussions.

Recruit a volunteer to read 'The Fruit Bowl' poem and ask for comments and feedback. Did the students enjoy the rhyme? Were there other rhymes that may have fitted? Could this have been written as a non-rhyming poem?

Look at the 'finding rhymes' sheets, either word or picture versions, and allow learners some individual task time to identify rhymes. Once again, discuss findings as a group, assessing if your learners found this challenging or easy.

Now move on to the poem templates. Ask students to make a choice about the four fruit supplied and hand out the appropriate template. Make learners aware that there is more than one suitable word for the end of each line (some rhyming and some non-rhyming). It's up to the student what sort of poem they wish to write. Some students may also want to find their own end words. Regroup and encourage students to read out and share their work with each other. How do the poems change when non-rhyming endings are used? Does the meaning of the sentence stay the same/make sense?

Differentiation and development

- You may choose to bring in a selection of rhyming poetry for the group to study and give their feedback on; this can be pitched to the ability and language level of the learners and could be about their own favourite topic. They may have access to the means to conduct their own research to find preferred poems on the internet.

- For students not working with written language, develop work with the picture versions of the finding rhymes sheets. These students could go on to identify verbally rhyming words for the other pictures on the sheet and work at putting two rhyming words into a sentence. For example, 'the coat was left on the boat'.

- Supply magazines for students to cut out and pair up rhyming words.

- This poetry activity complements Activity 2.5.

- Students could develop creative work by taking photographs of the fruit from various stages of whole to cut, distant, close up and arranged shots.

The Fruit Bowl

A collection of offerings...huddled, cuddled...bundled

in a bowl,

Hugging to each other, filling spaces, making one form

One picture, one whole.

Scented, exotic, thick skins and thin,

Sturdy and fragile all textures mixed in.

No angles, no edges, just spheres and curves, shiny and dull.

One round container, spilling with colours heavy and full.

Find words that rhyme and join with a *line!*

Spread Sour Sweet Fed Heat Red Mellow Best Queen Pay Zest Yellow Loose Treat Tower Clean Juice

What rhymes with...?

Circle the picture that rhymes with the one in the thought cloud.

What rhymes with...?

Circle the picture that rhymes with the one in the thought cloud.

What rhymes with...?

Circle the picture that rhymes with the one in the thought cloud.

What rhymes with...?

Circle the picture that rhymes with the one in the thought cloud.

The Jacket

A strangely bent fruit with a cheeky curve

It must feel the cold as it waits to be _____

Wearing several coats from green to brown

But the yellow one wins the tastiest _____

Hugging together with its friends in a hand

Shipped from a warm and exotic _____

Its jacket protects it from bumps and scrapes

But never keeps out the monkeys and _____

Pluck him, peel him and take off the sun suit

To sink your teeth into the soft white _____

Fill in the poem above with rhyming or non-rhyming endings.

picked, land, crown, chimps, flesh,

served, skin, place, taste, medal,

prize, apes, fruit

Zest and Zing

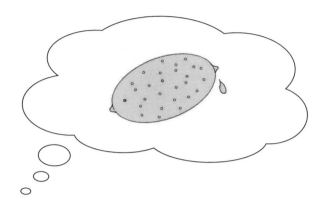

He sits in the bowl in his dimpled skin

Glossy and yellow, then he starts to _____

'Tears to the eyes I like to bring

with my zip and my tang and my zest and _____ ,

He's a strange little fruit all sharp and sour

Not really one to chomp and _____

But a drip or drizzle just here and there

Can perk up the dullest of culinary _____

So we'll leave the happy chap in the bowl to sing

As he boasts of his zip and his tang and his _____

Fill in the poem above with rhyming or non-rhyming endings.

ring, boast, pith, skin,

chew, dishes, sing, zing,

devour, fare, share

Peculiar Prickles

Where does it come from with its spiky hat?

Its prickly body all round and _____

How does it grow...on the ground...off the tree?

How do I open it to eat it for _____?

Will it taste sweet or be sharp and sour?

Can I prepare it in less than an _____?

What colour resides in your rusty shell?

So many questions I have to _____

There's only one way to know what you provide

Take off your hat and peek _____

Fill in the poem above with rhyming or non-rhyming endings.

inside, tea, minute, chunky,

say, skin, fat, lunch, tell,

prize, hour, within, ask

A Midnight Snack

An apple...red, crisp and round

Fell fast and quietly to the _____

It landed, thud in a pile of leaves

Left to be taken by bandits and _____

And sure enough they came in the night

To sniff and lick and take a _____

From the apple, red, crisp and round

That fell fast and quietly to the _____

First came the owl then the mouse then the vole

Till along came a fox who crunched it _____

Fill in the poem above with rhyming or non-rhyming endings.

floor, ground, grass, land,

robbers, elves, thieves,

bite, crunch, taste, nibble, gulp,

down, whole, fast, loud

4.4 Storytelling
Take a Picture, Weave a Narrative

This whole group story-creating exercise is designed to get students exercising their full communication repertoires – spoken, signed and gestured – to come together to create an imaginative short story. It will also motivate listening skills when the story is read back and students will be asked to listen out for their element. The theme extends beyond, but still includes, our fruit bowl images and language, and if this activity is preceded by the others in this section then your students will be furnished with lots of adjectives to describe the fruit elements of the story. I find my students like to go down the 'silly story' route; it often evokes more language, more laughter and keeps listeners on board.

Aims

- Increase awareness of others members of the group.
- Develop imagination skills.
- Practise language and communication skills.
- Create the opportunity to construct a spoken narrative.
- Create the opportunity to express creative ideas.

Resources

- A set of the story pictures printed onto white card.

- A large sheet of paper and flip chart or a projector and laptop for the session leader to write the story on for the group to see.

Prior to the activity

- Print off picture cards.

- Gather resources for any differentiated activities (see below).

Delivering the activity

Lead a discussion about fiction stories… Who likes them, and what sort (serious, funny, fantasy, ghost, detective, romance, etc.)? Describe how a story can just evolve once you get started and isn't quite as difficult to write once ideas get flowing and lots of people contribute.

Place the picture cards face down in the middle of the table and ask for a volunteer to start the story by turning one card over. They may just label the picture, for example 'dancing', and will need supportive questions to help construct a starting sentence – who was dancing? What are their names? What day of the week was it?

The starting sentence may look like this, 'One Saturday night Susan and Tom had gone dancing…' Take into account ideas from the rest of the group and once the first sentence is agreed it is written up by the session leader onto a flip chart or typed up and projected. The next card is turned over. Then your next student may turn over, for example, 'banana' and the story may evolve into 'One Saturday night Susan and Tom had gone dancing…to the Straight Banana Party Club', or '…they stopped to drink a refreshing iced banana cocktail', or '…they left in their yellow mini that they'd nicknamed Banana Betty'. Get the picture? Sentences can be as long, or as short, or as sensible, or as silly as the ideas that the pictures produce.

Support students to connect their ideas so that each sentence links to the next and as you get to the last couple of picture cards remind students that the story is going to be drawing to a close.

When the final work is written up, make sure each student has a copy of the picture card they used to contribute their own sentence. Now read the work out to the group and as each learner hears their own part they can hold their picture up. Students will enjoy having a typed-up copy of the story to take home. Remind the group that story writing is fun and can be easier than they think if they just look around them for inspiration.

Differentiation and development

- Students working at a higher level of literacy may enjoy writing their own stories using a set of their own picture cards; select ten images from the internet/magazines that may appeal to individuals.

- If the group are working quickly and coming up with lots of ideas you could go around the table twice so that each picture element is woven into the story twice before the story concludes.

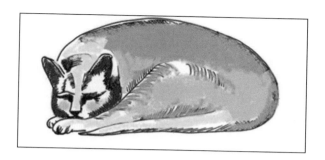